MARY MAC'S
TEA ROOM

Mary Mac's Tea Room

Thursday, May 6, 1971

LUNCHEON

Prices Below Include Georgia State Sale Tax

No. 1 — 1.85

ROAST SIRLOIN OF WESTERN BEEF with BROWN GRAVY
Choice of Two Vegetables, Dessert, Coffee or Tea

No. 2 — 1.65

BAKED CHICKEN AND DRESSING
(ALL WHITE MEAT .50 EXTRA)
Choice of Two Vegetables, Dessert, Coffee or Tea

No. 3 — 1.45

BAKED SWISS STEAK
ALL BEEF MEAT LOAF with TOMATO SAUCE
OLD FASHION STEWED CHICKEN AND DUMPLINGS
CHICKEN PAN PIE
Choice of Two Vegetables, Dessert, Coffee or Tea

No. 4 — 1.30

SPAGHETTI WITH ITALIAN MEAT SAUCE, PARMESAN CHEESE
STEAMED FRANKFURTERS WITH SAUERKRAUT

Welcome to
MARY MAC'S
Tea Room

MARY MAC'S TEA ROOM

65 Years of Recipes from
Atlanta's Favorite Dining Room

JOHN FERRELL

Foreword by

MARIE LUPO NYGREN

Andrews McMeel
Publishing, LLC
Kansas City • Sydney • London

10 11 12 13 14 TWP 10 9 8 7 6 5 4 3 2 1

ISBN-13: 978-0-7407-9338-7
ISBN-10: 0-7407-9338-1

Library of Congress Control Number: 2009943092

Design: Pinafore Press / Janice Shay
Photography: Deborah Whitlaw Llewellyn
Additional photography: Brad Newton, pages ii, v, 19, 128, 169

www.andrewsmcmeel.com
www.marymacs.com

ATTENTION: SCHOOLS AND BUSINESSES

Andrews McMeel books are available at quantity discounts with
bulk purchase for educational, business, or sales promotional
use. For information, please write to: Special Sales Department,
Andrews McMeel Publishing, LLC, 1130 Walnut Street, Kansas
City, Missouri 64106.

THIS BOOK IS DEDICATED TO my loving parents John and Mary Ferrell who found and adopted me at birth. Without their unconditional love, encouragement, and support, I would not be where I am today. John and Mary are now gone, but they are in my thoughts daily and greatly missed. Their unique parenting taught me many things about love, learning, and life. I was raised to respect all people, especially my elders. I learned at a very early age to say "thank you" and mean it. I was taught not to be heard but to listen—and to always tell the truth. I can honestly say that my parents would be grateful for this virtue and the fact that I try to live by the golden rule. When I turned fifty a few years ago, I realized that I had somehow managed to inherit the same trait my father complained of having: never knowing what or when something is going to come out of my mouth! My good friends Ruth and Ruby Crawford gave me a solution for my problem with their mother's wise advice to them—"Always tell the truth . . . but don't always be telling it."

Thanks also to my partner, Hank Thompson, who came into my life just before my fiftieth birthday. Hank is one of the happiest people I have ever met and a perfect complement to my life and to Mary Mac's. We often feel that our mothers—who knew their boys well—must have met in heaven and had a wonderful time planning our life together as the perfect match! We have many things in common, including being adopted and growing up as the only child in a very loving home. We both grew up in small communities in the South, and were raised with the same values instilled in us by our parents. Of course, we both love Southern food, and while some people may eat to live, we live to eat!

Hank's love for Mary Mac's Tea Room, his keen business sense, and his unique ability to listen and solve problems, as well as being able to motivate me and the staff, are a constant blessing. I have the best business partner a man could have . . . all thanks to our sweet mamas, Mary and Alice!

My secret hope is that one or both of Hank's children, Matthew and Shannon, will share our love of Mary Mac's and its legacy and will continue its storied history long after we are gone.

—JOHN FERRELL

BREAD (Please circle choice)
Yeast Rolls   Cornbread   All

DESSERT

BEVERAGE
10

BAR
11 Wine   12 Beer   13 Liquor

CUSTOMER
NAME
Dine In   •   Take Out   •   Catering   •   Banquets

Mary Mac's
TEA ROOM

224 Ponce de Leon Ave., N.E.
Atlanta, Georgia 30308
Phone: (404) 876-1800
FAX: (404) 881-6003

MARIE LUPO NYGREN ON MARY MAC'S

My mother, Margaret Lupo, began her story with Mary Mac's in the early 1960s, just after her own tea room, Margaret's Tray Shop, in the heart of downtown, closed. A week after Mother started working at Mary Mac's, the owner, Mary McKinsey, announced she was getting married and moving to Florida, and asked Mother to buy the business. Mother agreed to the offer, and was again in the tea room business.

At that time, there were several tea rooms in Atlanta. They had been opened by ladies as a way to make extra money, and the name was a misnomer, as it wasn't a place to have tea, but a nicer version of a "meat and three." It appealed to people who had moved to Atlanta from small towns in Georgia because it reminded them of their mom's cooking.

One of the beauties of Mary Mac's was that everyone was welcome; it wasn't an exclusive dining room like so many in Atlanta were at that time. At one table, you would see the mayor or the governor. At the next table, there might be a group of Atlanta workers. Mother welcomed everyone, regardless of race. Segregation was at the forefront in Atlanta in the early '60s, but Mother made it clear from the start that "everyone's money is the same color, and if you don't understand that, then you don't need to work in my restaurant." She

never tolerated disrespect, and was affectionately known as "Mama" to her staff and guests. She treated that dining room as if it were her own personal dining room.

Mary Mac's was always a microcosm of culture, reflecting the mood and trends of society. In the early '70s, when Atlanta became the hot spot for the hippie culture, they all camped out at 10th and Peachtree, and they'd eat at Mary Mac's. Then when Atlanta became the gay mecca, all the boys came to eat with "Mama." And Mother loved it, and loved them all. I grew up at what many would consider an ideal family table: a little bit of everything was represented.

At Mother's funeral, the Reverend Austin Ford said Mary Mac's was the "political salon of Atlanta." I'd never thought of it quite that way, but it truly was.

Mother took me to work at an early age—first, I got passed hip to hip in the kitchen, then my first job at the age of six was to dry the silver. I graduated to cashier when I was nine, and became a hostess when I was fifteen.

Because so many politicians dined at Mary Mac's, Mother kept up to date on the issues and became quite politically active. She wanted to instill a sense of community activism in me, and she knew that working at the restaurant would introduce me to this world. She enlisted me to campaign for Charles Weltner when he campaigned for U.S. congressman, and I remember passing out flyers and campaigning on the street. I was twelve years old.

Just as Mother demanded respect and tolerance in the dining room, she demanded freshness in the kitchen. Mother never used a canned vegetable. My father, Harvey Lupo, was a produce wholesaler, and was in charge of buying for Mary Mac's. He and I would make twice-weekly trips to the state farmers' market and load up the van. Back at the restaurant, the kitchen would be shucking bushels of corn, and it was not an unusual sight to see the bartender shucking corn and snapping beans between serving customers. In a week, we'd go through 25 bushels of corn, 25 bushels of green beans, 25 bushels of collards and turnip greens.

At the height of its popularity, Mary Mac's was serving 2,000 people a day. That's a lot of collards and green beans. And since Mother always insisted on fresh vegetables, that's how my appreciation and love for farm-fresh food began.

I'm thrilled that someone with equal passion for good Southern food is now at the helm at Mary Mac's, and I'm proud to have played a role in it. I first met John in 1978 when we were students at Florida State University. Our friendship continued as my husband, Steve, became John's mentor in the restaurant industry. When Mother decided to sell, Steve and I both thought John was the perfect fit to carry on the storied tradition of this iconic Atlanta establishment. I approached him with the idea, then brought John to the table with Mother to start the conversation. She agreed with our thinking, and I'm sure she would still be happy that John has kept the traditions of Mary Mac's alive and healthy.

Today, I am the owner of The Farmhouse at the Inn at Serenbe, which is my own version of an upscale "meat and three." When my husband and I founded the Serenbe community, it was important that we have an organic farm—not only because we wanted access to food grown without chemicals and with love, but because we also knew that food binds a community together, and we wanted to give the families at Serenbe the magical experience we'd had growing food together as a family. When people come to my restaurant, I still feel they are coming to dine in my personal dining room. And they are treated just as my mother would have wanted me to treat them.

—*Marie Lupo Nygren*, November 2009

KEEPING THE MARY MAC'S TRADITION ALIVE

It is a huge responsibility to run a restaurant that is both a landmark and a piece of Atlanta's history—and one that I happily shoulder. Mary Mac's Tea Room is not only the story of a restaurant that has served diners for more than sixty-five years, it is a story that plays out over decades and includes founders, family, friends, employees, and, most of all, our loyal customers.

The question I hear most often is, "What's it like to own this place?" The answer is simple: Mary Mac's is a merry-go-round! All you can do is think fast, jump in, and hang on, day after day. The restaurant has gathered its own momentum over the last sixty-five years and has a rhythm and life all its own.

You never really own a timeless place like Mary Mac's, you just take care of its legacy and treasures. I'm constantly reminded of this by one of the old framed menus on our walls—dated a week before I was born in 1956. It gives me pause each time I see that menu, to realize that the restaurant existed even before I did.

So, you understand, I am not the founder of Mary Mac's Tea Room, but its present owner. It began with a woman named Mary McKinsey, and was passed on to Margaret Lupo, who successfully ran it for thirty years. (The early chapters of this book recount the history of the first four decades of business at Mary Mac's.)

It was Margaret Lupo's willingness to sell me her venerable business, share her knowledge, and lend her guidance that has made my chapter possible in the Mary Mac's story. For that I am truly grateful. Mrs. Lupo's daughter, Marie, and Marie's husband, Steve Nygren, have given me endless encouragement, helping me get through both the good days and the bad days. Mrs. Lupo's other daughters, Barbara Trieglaff and Judy Wold, have also generously encouraged me.

My mother and father, Mary Ferrell and John Ferrell Sr. were both proud to pitch in and give me their support when I bought Mary Mac's. They enjoyed the excitement of the place and all the new people they got to meet, although I think they must've secretly wondered whether I'd gone completely crazy to take on such a formidable task. My father liked to visit from his home in Florida. He knew how to tell a story with a grin and a laugh, and the customers loved him. Not too many years ago, he began making the pepper sauce for the restaurant, a spicy concoction that perfectly matched his personality.

When I first walked into Mary Mac's as owner in 1994, I had a long "to do" list full of details that had to be completed before we could reopen the restaurant. Thank goodness I also had a list of good and faithful friends.

They lent encouragement and more, with many of them volunteering their time to help clean, scrub, and shine the place up. When I walk around Mary Mac's now, I can still see the clean glow of their elbow grease and feel the warmth of their good wishes.

When you spend time at Mary Mac's, you meet a lot of people who love it. Many of these folks who are "friends of the restaurant" have become friends of mine, too, and I thank them for their loyal support. You will read about Judge Dorothy Beasley, who brings in new customers from around the globe to experience a taste of the South and a dose of our hospitality.

Former senator Max Cleland is always a cheerful and welcome presence in the dining room and I still remember and appreciate the big hug and kiss his late mother gave me each time she would come for lunch. I also appreciated the delicious vine-ripened tomatoes Senator Cleland's father brought me from his summer garden.

On average, Mary Mac's serves more than 1,000 meals a day, and a large portion of those meals are served to a lunchtime rush crowd that includes many of Atlanta's businessmen and women. When Doug Ivester was named CEO of Coca-Cola, he did us the huge honor of telling the *Atlanta Journal-Constitution* that Mary Mac's was his favorite restaurant. I appreciate the patronage and support that our many lunchtime business customers have given us over the years.

When you look around the restaurant at lunch—or later, at dinner—you're likely to see a complete cross section of the Atlanta community, which is several million strong. Given Atlanta's numerous international visitors, I sometimes believe I see the entire world come through our doors. Everybody likes good food, and our mission at Mary Mac's is to serve good Southern food to everybody.

Over the years, Mary Mac's loyal and talented employees have helped the restaurant grow and prosper. They're the friendly faces of Mary Mac's, and they keep our customers smiling.

My kitchen angel, Flora Hunter, has been cooking our delicious soufflés, chicken and dumplings, cornbread dressing, meat loaf, bread pudding, and banana pudding for thirty-five years and is still going strong!

Flo Patrick has been a server for thirty-seven years. She has many regular customers who only want to sit and eat in her station. Flo hit the big time a few years back with her photo in the travel section of the *New York Times*, planting a big kiss on one of our customers.

Evelyn Stewart started out as the bartender thirty-five years ago and is now a beloved server. Senator Max Cleland and his family are some of Evelyn's "regulars."

Martha Evans, a thirty-seven-year veteran server, is known for her outrageous earrings and friendly smile. Martha loves to talk and will happily tell you about some of the interesting customers she's had over the years. Like the one who always wanted his cornbread heated so hot that it was burned around the edges, or the ornery one who told her to stop calling him "darlin'"!

Shirley Mitchell has baked our yeast rolls, cornbread, peach cobbler, and cinnamon rolls for more than three decades, and is still baking up sweet magic in the kitchen.

Jo Carter welcomes customers at the door and gives her famous back rubs table-to-table. She's our happy "goodwill ambassador."

All of our employees play their part, and I've dedicated an entire chapter to them in this book, so you'll hear more about the people who make Mary Mac's an Atlanta institution.

I'm pleased to be able to bring you these recipes from Mary Mac's Tea Room. I hope they remind you of the best in home cooking and that we see you in Mary Mac's very soon.

APPETIZERS

Plus a little bit

of history

about how it

all started

HISTORY

MARY MAC'S TEA ROOM is the last of sixteen tea rooms that once dotted intown Atlanta in the 1940s. The food is undeniably comforting, the atmosphere feels as familiar as your grandmother's kitchen, and the waitstaff treats every customer as if they were serving their long-lost cousin a holiday meal.

Traditions are important to life in the South, and not many things have changed at the Atlanta landmark since it opened its doors in 1945. The location has stayed the same, and the food, cooked fresh daily, remains nearly identical to what it was sixty-five years ago. From macaroni and cheese to fried chicken and sweet potato soufflé, the kitchen serves many of the same classic Southern recipes that have been on the menu for decades. Guests are sometimes greeted with a friendly "Hey, honey, how are ya?" spoken with the requisite Southern accent.

When you're seated at a table, you'll notice the pencils and order forms with which to write your own order—a custom that has endured for six decades. During your meal, Mary Mac's "goodwill ambassador," Jo Carter, may stop by your table to chat and give you a back rub if she thinks you're looking too stressed. No customer ever leaves Mary Mac's unnoticed— you can be sure of it.

Dining at Mary Mac's has become a rite of passage for every first-time visitor to Atlanta, too. Each new guest receives a complimentary cup of pot likker and a piece of cornbread. For those not fortunate enough to be raised on such Southern delicacies, the servers explain that the cornbread should be crumbled into the bowl of broth. They are also happy to explain exactly what pot likker is for those customers from above the Mason-Dixon Line. Don't worry; there's more about that in a later chapter.

Many restaurants in this vast city do a good business feeding anonymous customers who come and go, never to be seen again. Such is the size and "busy-ness" of Atlanta. At Mary Mac's, regulars dine there weekly—some even daily. Atlantans have made Mary Mac's a part of their lives for generations. Crowds stream

It wasn't uncommon for widows to open tea rooms and serve the food Southern women knew how to cook best. They called their establishments "tea rooms," rather than using the more pedestrian-sounding "restaurant," as a way of making the business seem instantly respectable.

through the doors on Sundays after church for the traditional Sunday dinner. Others eat lunch during the workday and bring their families back at night. It's not just a place to eat; it has been Atlanta's dining room for a long while.

The many framed pieces that cover the dining room walls create a sense of nostalgia, even for first-time customers. Walking by the hundreds of photographs, articles, awards, and letters of thanks creates a bridge to the past—both Mary Mac's past and that of this great Southern city. Most longtime customers take the time to glance around the walls each visit, checking for any new additions to the "scrapbook gallery."

Along with the treasured photographs of regular customers and friends, there are the celebrities and famous faces that have graced the tables over the years. Musicians such as

James Brown, country music star Alan Jackson, Beyoncé, and Cher; politicians and leaders, including former first lady Hillary Rodham Clinton, Senator Max Cleland, a slew of Georgia governors, and the Dalai Lama; business and industry tycoons; educator William Suttles, and the group of Georgia Tech professors who eat at Mary Mac's daily; and so many stage and film stars that it is hard to count the pictures.

The tea room has lived through five owners; a series of expansions; a few robberies; endless political events and famous visits; countless weddings; and hundreds of meetings, church functions, and family reunions. Mary Mac's history rivals the richness of its macaroni and cheese and reflects Atlanta's meteoric rise to become the unofficial capital of the South.

At the midpoint of the twentieth century, Ponce de Leon Avenue presented a much

different scene then than today. The Pig & Whistle served burgers at the spot where Krispy Kreme serves up its famous hot doughnuts now. The Atlanta Crackers baseball team played to enthusiastic crowds at their rickety ballpark on the spot of today's Midtown Home Depot nearby. Watermelon tents served ice-cold watermelon on tables nestled in piles of sawdust. Clanking trolley cars guided by a web of tracks transported Atlantans to destinations too far to walk. Ornate movie palaces such as the Fox Theatre, Atlanta Theatre, and Loew's Grand showed first-run films to packed houses.

Atlanta's neighborhood restaurants were a familiar feature for residents of the city. Many of them were known as "tea rooms," and in the 1940s and '50s they were the centers of neighborhood camaraderie. For many Atlantans, tea rooms became the place where families enjoyed a familiar welcome, good food, and the company of their friends and neighbors.

In the late 1940s, Mrs. Fuller's Tea Room, on Ponce de Leon Avenue, was a small but dependable feature in midtown Atlanta. Along with Crawford Long Hospital, the local drugstore, the filling stations, grocery stores, and churches along the Ponce corridor, a community was easily accessible for the residents of the area.

But Mrs. Fuller was eager to sell her business. Over time, several people bought it, only to default after a short time in business. All the while, Mary McKinsey, who ran a restaurant on 17th Street called the Rose Bowl Tea Room, had her eye on Mrs. Fuller's. After watching several others try and fail at running the place, she finally bought Mrs. Fuller's Tea Room in 1951. McKinsey vowed to succeed, and with hard work she did thrive. She kept

Mrs. Fuller's name out front for about a year, then in 1953, she changed the name to Mary Mac's Tea Room, and a legend was born.

Not much is known about the personal life of Mary McKinsey, but Margaret Lupo described her as "a big redheaded woman with a hearty laugh and a lot of personality." Best of all, she could produce good food and good service, and Mary Mac's flourished.

When Mary McKinsey took charge of the tea room, could she ever have imagined that it would outlive all other tea rooms in Atlanta and that its reputation would stretch around the world? Probably not, since she was motivated by far more immediate concerns. A widow, she did what many other widows were forced to do in the postwar years— found a way to make a living and support herself and her family. It wasn't uncommon for widows to open tea rooms and serve the food Southern women knew how to cook best. They called their establishments "tea rooms," rather than using the more pedestrian-sounding "restaurant," as a way of making the business seem instantly respectable. Mind you, there were no teapots in sight and the only tea served would be sweet Southern iced tea—and that wasn't even on the menu until many years later!

The tea rooms of the late 1940s were often located close to one another. In the same quickly growing area near downtown and the newly popular apartment houses along Ponce de Leon Avenue, Piedmont Avenue boasted the Piedmont Tea Room and nearby on Peachtree Street was the Peachtree Tea Room.

Then, in 1962, news came that Mary Mac's Tea Room, an established seventy-five-seat restaurant, needed a new owner. Mary McKinsey planned to leave Atlanta and get married. Margaret Lupo jumped at the

MARGARET LUPO

opportunity. The Lupos and Mary McKinsey had been good friends for years. Mary knew about Margaret's previous experience in restaurant life and trusted that she was the best candidate to take over her business. The deal was made.

THE CITY OF ATLANTA GREW RAPIDLY AFTER WORLD WAR II, BUT DOWNTOWN DID NOT YET PRESENT THE SKYLINE OF IMPRESSIVE SKYSCRAPERS IT HAS TODAY. THIS VIEW DOWN PONCE DE LEON AVENUE, JUST BLOCKS FROM MARY MAC'S TEA ROOM AND DOWNTOWN, REVEALS NO TALL BUILDINGS YET ON THE HORIZON. BOTTOM LEFT: MARGARET MITCHELL, ATLANTA AUTHOR OF *GONE WITH THE WIND*, HAD SEEN THE MOVIE VERSION OF HER BOOK PREMIERE IN 1939 AT A THEATER NEAR THE INTERSEC-TION OF PONCE DE LEON AND PEACHTREE. MITCHELL'S COUSIN, MARGARET LUPO, WOULD BUY MARY MAC'S TEA ROOM IN 1962. BOTTOM RIGHT: THESE ARE THE SMALL STOREFRONTS THAT, ONE BY ONE, WERE BOUGHT BY MARGARET LUPO AND BECAME PART OF THE MARY MAC'S RESTAURANT.

CRANBERRY PECAN SALAD

SERVES 8 TO 10

This recipe comes from my partner Hank's aunt, who resides in Bardstown, Kentucky.

1 ¹/₂ cups granulated sugar	²/₃ cup chopped pecans
1 ¹/₄ cups water	1 cup diced celery
4 cups fresh cranberries	1 large Granny Smith apple, peeled,
2 tablespoons (2 packages) plain gelatin	cored, and diced
1 tablespoon freshly squeezed lemon juice	Grapes and orange sections, for garnish

Oil a 2-quart mold or glass baking dish.

Bring the sugar and 1 cup of the water to a boil in a saucepan over medium-high heat and cook for about 5 minutes, or until the sugar is dissolved. Add the cranberries and cook until the skins burst. Cook for about 5 minutes; remove from the heat.

Soften the gelatin in the remaining ¹/₄ cup cold water and add to the cranberries, stirring until dissolved. Add the lemon juice and let cool slightly. When the mixture begins to thicken, 5 to 7 minutes, fold in the pecans, celery, and apple.

Place in the mold or glass baking dish and chill for at least 6 hours. Remove from the mold and garnish with grapes and orange sections.

BATTERED CORNMEAL FRIES

SERVES 4

We often serve these fries as an appetizer or with a meal. They are a yummy change from French fries, and the cornmeal adds a Southern twist.

1/2 cup whole milk

1 1/2 teaspoons sugar

1 1/2 teaspoons salt

1/2 teaspoon freshly ground black pepper

4 large russet potatoes, scrubbed and skin
    left on, julienned into 1/4-inch sticks

Peanut oil

1/2 cup cornmeal

1/2 cup all-purpose flour

Line a plate with paper towels and set aside.

In a flat-bottomed dish, combine the milk, 1 teaspoon of the sugar, 1 teaspoon of the salt, and 1/4 teaspoon of the pepper. Add the julienned potatoes and soak for 15 minutes. Pour peanut oil into a large cast-iron skillet to a depth of 2 inches and heat to 360°F.

Combine the cornmeal, the flour, the remaining 1/2 teaspoon sugar, the remaining 1/2 teaspoon salt, and the remaining 1/4 teaspoon of the pepper in a paper bag. Drain the potatoes, discarding the milk, place in the bag, and shake until well coated.

Fry in batches for 3 to 4 minutes, until golden brown and tender on the inside. Drain on the plate. Serve immediately.

BLACK-EYED PEA CAKES

SERVES 4 TO 6

2 cups cooked black-eyed peas (page 14), chilled

1 cup diced yellow onions

1/2 cup all-purpose flour

1 teaspoon salt

1 teaspoon freshly ground black pepper

1 teaspoon sugar

1 teaspoon baking powder

2 large eggs

Vegetable oil

1 tablespoon finely chopped cilantro plus 1 tablespoon for garnish

Line a plate with paper towels and set aside.

Place the black-eyed peas and onions in a mixing bowl. Using a potato masher, mash until chunky with a few whole peas remaining. Add the flour, salt, pepper, sugar, and baking powder and mix well. Add the eggs and mix well. Stir in 1 tablespoon of the cilantro and mix well.

Heat 1/4 inch of oil in a large, heavy skillet over medium-high heat. Form the mixture into 3-inch patties. Fry in batches in hot oil for 3 to 4 minutes on each side, until golden brown. Transfer to the plate. Repeat the procedure with the remaining patties. Garnish with the remaining 1 tablespoon cilantro.

CARROT-RAISIN SALAD

SERVES 6 TO 8

7 large carrots, peeled and shredded

1 cup raisins

1/2 cup mayonnaise

1/3 cup confectioners' sugar

Combine all the ingredients in a large bowl. Refrigerate for at least 1 hour before serving.

COLE SLAW

SERVES 6 TO 8

1 head green cabbage, cored and
   shredded

1/2 large carrot, peeled and shredded

2 cups mayonnaise

1/2 cup confectioners' sugar

1 teaspoon salt

1 teaspoon white pepper

Toss together the cabbage and carrot in a large bowl. Add the mayonnaise and the remaining ingredients and stir until blended. Refrigerate for at least 1 hour before serving.

BRUNSWICK STEW

SERVES 4

There are some that claim this traditional Southern stew was first created in Brunswick County, Virginia. In Georgia, we know, without a doubt, that Brunswick stew was invented in Brunswick, Georgia, on July 2, 1898.

2 cups finely chopped barbecued pulled pork

1 cup finely chopped cooked chicken

2 tablespoons salted butter

1 cup chopped yellow onions

1 (14 1/2-ounce) can crushed tomatoes, undrained

1 (5-ounce) can whole kernel corn, drained

1/4 teaspoon salt

1/4 teaspoon freshly ground black pepper

Dash of hot sauce

Dash of Worcestershire sauce

2 tablespoons Barbecue Sauce (page 44)

Combine the pork and chicken in a bowl; set aside. In a stockpot or Dutch oven, melt the butter over medium-high heat and sauté the onions until soft and translucent, 3 to 4 minutes. Add the tomatoes and corn; cook for 5 minutes. Add the pork and chicken; reduce the heat, cover, and simmer for 1 hour.

Add the salt, pepper, hot sauce, Worcestershire sauce, and barbecue sauce to the pot. If the stew is too thick, add water to reach the desired consistency.

BLACK-EYED PEA SALAD

SERVES 6 TO 8

Mrs. Lupo's daughter, Marie Lupo Nygren, provided me with this tasty recipe and I have often used it at parties for an appetizer. The secret is to marinate and chill the salad for at least 4 hours before serving.

1 pound dried black-eyed peas

3 tablespoons chopped fresh basil

2 red bell peppers, diced

2 green bell peppers, diced

1 medium red onion, halved and sliced
   thinly crosswise

1 teaspoon freshly ground black pepper

1/2 cup Champagne or other sparkling
   wine

1/2 cup rice wine vinegar

1/3 cup vegetable oil

1 teaspoon salt (optional)

Place the black-eyed peas in a stockpot and add water to cover. Soak overnight.

Drain the peas, rinse, and return to the pot; cover with water. Bring to a boil over medium-high heat and cook until tender, about 1 hour. Drain and rinse with cold water. Let cool completely.

In a large bowl, combine the basil, red and green bell peppers, red onion, and black pepper. Add the cooled peas and mix well.

In a small bowl, combine the Champagne, rice wine vinegar, and vegetable oil; pour over the vegetables. Sprinkle with the salt. Chill for 4 to 5 hours before serving.

CUCUMBERS WITH SOUR CREAM DRESSING

SERVES 4

2 medium cucumbers, peeled and sliced
   into rounds
1 large sweet onion, sliced into rings and
   separated
1/4 cup sugar

1/4 teaspoon salt
1/8 teaspoon freshly ground black pepper
1/2 cup mayonnaise
2 tablespoons white vinegar
3 tablespoons whole milk

Place the cucumbers in a large bowl. Add the onion. Add 1 tablespoon of the sugar, the salt, and pepper and toss to combine. In a separate bowl, combine the mayonnaise, the remaining 3 tablespoons sugar, the vinegar, and milk. Pour the dressing over the cucumber mixture and toss to coat. Chill for at least 1 hour before serving.

DADDY'S OYSTER STEW

SERVES 4 TO 6

When I grew up, my family lived close to the Gulf of Mexico and it was always a treat when oyster season arrived. We would make our annual pilgrimage to the coast to retrieve the famous Apalachicola oysters. I still like to cook with these oysters whenever I get the chance.

4 tablespoons (1/2 stick) unsalted butter

1 medium sweet or yellow onion, minced

1 clove garlic, minced

1/4 teaspoon salt

1/4 teaspoon freshly ground black pepper

1 pint fresh raw oysters, juices reserved

4 cups whole milk

Salt and freshly ground black pepper

In a medium saucepan, melt 2 tablespoons of the butter over medium-high heat. Sauté the onion and garlic, stirring occasionally, until the onion is soft and translucent, 3 to 4 minutes. Add the salt and pepper. Add the oysters and their juices and cook just until the oysters look opaque and the edges begin to curl.

Reduce the heat to medium-low and add the milk. Cut the remaining 2 tablespoons butter into 2 pieces and add to the pan. Stir until the butter is melted (do not boil); remove the pan from the heat. Add salt and pepper to taste and serve with fresh saltine crackers.

FRESH CORN AND BACON CHOWDER

SERVES 4 TO 6

8 ears fresh corn

4 slices bacon

1/2 cup finely chopped sweet onion

1/2 cup thinly sliced celery

1 cup water

2 cups whole milk

1 teaspoon sugar

1 teaspoon dried thyme

1/2 teaspoon salt

1/4 teaspoon freshly ground black pepper

2 teaspoons cornstarch

Line a plate with paper towels and set aside.

Cut off the tops of the kernels of corn into a bowl. Scrape the corn milk and remaining pulp from each cob with a paring knife into the same bowl and set aside. In a large Dutch oven over medium heat, cook the bacon until crisp. Drain the bacon on a plate, reserving 2 tablespoons of the drippings in the Dutch oven. When cooled, crumble the bacon and set aside.

Cook the onion and celery in the reserved bacon drippings over medium-high heat, stirring frequently, until tender, 5 to 7 minutes. Stir in the corn, corn milk, and water. Bring to a boil; cover, reduce the heat, and simmer for 10 minutes, stirring occasionally.

Stir in 1 1/2 cups of the milk, the sugar, thyme, salt, and pepper and cook over low heat. Combine the cornstarch and the remaining 1/2 cup milk and stir until smooth. Gradually add the cornstarch mixture to the corn mixture, stirring constantly until dissolved. Cover and cook for 10 minutes, stirring often, until thickened and bubbly. Sprinkle with the crumbled bacon to serve.

FRIED EGGPLANT STRIPS

SERVES 6

I medium eggplant, peeled and cut into
   1/4-inch-wide by 2-inch-long strips

I 1/2 teaspoons salt

I cup all-purpose flour

I large egg, lightly beaten

I cup whole milk

Vegetable oil

Line a plate with paper towels and set aside.

Place the eggplant strips in a bowl; add I teaspoon of the salt and water to cover; let soak for I hour. Drain the eggplant and pat dry with paper towels. In a medium bowl, combine the flour and the remaining 1/2 teaspoon salt. Whisk together the egg, milk, and I tablespoon oil in a separate bowl.

Heat I inch of oil in a large, heavy skillet over medium-high heat. Dip the eggplant strips in the egg bath, then dredge in the flour mixture, shaking off the excess flour. Fry the eggplant strips in the hot oil until golden brown. Drain on the plate and serve hot.

Favorite Diners

Joe Patten, the Phantom of the Fox

Mr. Patten formed the Atlanta Landmarks, Inc., group in 1974 and almost single-handedly saved the Fox Theatre in downtown Atlanta from the wrecking ball. He was given an apartment within the theater for the remainder of his life (he's eighty-two now). He has eaten at Mary Mac's since 1953, when he first moved to Atlanta. It is a three-block walk from the theater to the restaurant, and he says he sometimes made the walk twice a day, for lunch and dinner. Patten has sent many visiting performers to Mary Mac's for the home cooking over the years. When he dines at Mary Mac's, the server Joe likes to "sit with" is Flo Carter.

FRIED OKRA

SERVES 4 TO 6

When I first bought Mary Mac's back in 1994, fried okra was served only one day a week and I was soon overwhelmed with requests for it the rest of the week. Now it's a permanent item on the menu.

2 cups vegetable oil

1 large egg, lightly beaten

1 tablespoon water

1 cup buttermilk

1 cup all-purpose flour

1 cup fine cracker crumbs

1½ teaspoons salt

½ teaspoon white pepper

1 pound okra, stemmed and sliced into ¼-inch pieces

Line a plate with paper towels and set aside.

Heat the oil to 350°F in a deep-fryer or deep, heavy skillet. Whisk together the egg, water, and buttermilk in a small bowl. In a paper bag, combine the flour, cracker crumbs, salt, and pepper.

Dip the okra into the buttermilk mixture, using a slotted spoon. Place the okra in the bag and shake until well coated. With another slotted spoon, remove the okra from the bag, shake gently to remove the excess flour, and place on a rack.

Fry the okra in the hot oil in batches until deep golden brown, 2 to 3 minutes. Drain on the plate, sprinkle with additional salt, if desired, and serve immediately.

GAZPACHO

SERVES 4 TO 6

1 large English cucumber, peeled, seeded, and coarsely chopped

3 large red tomatoes, peeled, seeded, and chopped

3/4 cup chopped sweet onion

1 clove garlic, minced

1 tablespoon minced fresh parsley

3/4 teaspoon ground cumin

1/4 teaspoon freshly ground black pepper

1/4 teaspoon salt

2 cups tomato juice

1/3 cup balsamic vinegar

Hot sauce

Place all the ingredients except the hot sauce in a blender or food processor and process until puréed. Add the hot sauce. Serve chilled.

POTATO SOUP

SERVES 4 TO 6

2 tablespoons olive oil

2 medium sweet onions, chopped

2 cloves garlic, minced

2 large stalks celery, chopped

4 medium white potatoes, peeled and cubed

1 teaspoon salt

1/2 teaspoon freshly ground black pepper

2 teaspoons finely chopped fresh basil

1/2 teaspoon poultry seasoning

6 cups chicken broth

4 tablespoons (1/2 stick) salted butter

1 cup sliced fresh mushrooms

Heat the olive oil in a large Dutch oven over medium-high heat. Sauté half of the onions, the garlic, and celery until the onions are soft and translucent. Add the remaining half of the onions, the potatoes, salt, pepper, basil, and poultry seasoning to the Dutch oven. Add the chicken broth and bring to a boil. Reduce the heat and simmer for 30 minutes, until the potatoes are tender.

Melt the butter in a medium sauté pan over medium-high heat. Add the mushrooms and cook until soft and beginning to brown. Add the mushrooms to the soup. Simmer for 15 minutes and serve.

RED POTATO SALAD

SERVES 4

2 1/2 pounds red potatoes, unpeeled and
 diced

6 hard-cooked eggs, peeled and chopped

I cup bread and butter pickles, diced

2 cups diced red onions

1/3 cup corn oil

2 cups mayonnaise

I tablespoon cider vinegar

1/2 teaspoon celery salt

1/2 teaspoon salt

1/4 teaspoon freshly ground black pepper

Place the diced potatoes in a stockpot and cover with water. Bring to a boil over medium-high heat; reduce the heat and simmer, cooking for about 15 minutes. Drain and let cool. Place in a large bowl; add the hard-cooked eggs, the diced pickles, and red onions, stirring to combine.

In a separate bowl, whisk together the oil, mayonnaise, vinegar, celery salt, salt, and pepper. Add to the potato mixture, mixing to combine. Refrigerate for several hours or overnight, until well chilled.

SHRIMP SALAD

SERVES 6 TO 8

3/4 cup mayonnaise

2 tablespoons Dijon mustard

I tablespoon sweet relish

2 teaspoons chopped fresh parsley

I tablespoon capers, drained

2 pounds large shrimp, boiled and peeled

I cup chopped green bell pepper

3/4 cup chopped celery

2 large red tomatoes, chopped

Salt and freshly ground black pepper

4 cups chopped lettuce or mixed greens

In a small bowl, combine the mayonnaise, Dijon mustard, relish, parsley, and capers.

In a large bowl, toss together the shrimp, the pepper, celery, and tomatoes. Add the dressing and toss to coat. Sprinkle with salt and pepper to taste. Divide the lettuce evenly among 4 plates and top with the shrimp mixture.

PESTO SAUCE

MAKES 3 (3-OUNCE) SERVINGS

Each serving is enough for two people. Not only is this a fantastic addition to pasta, fish and chicken, but it is equally enjoyable as an appetizer on toast. Freeze it for a quick and impressive appetizer at a later date.

6 cloves garlic, chopped

3 tablespoons salted butter, softened

3 tablespoons chopped walnuts

3 tablespoons pine nuts

1/2 teaspoon salt

1/2 teaspoon freshly ground black pepper

Pinch of ground nutmeg

1/4 cup loosely packed fresh parsley

2/3 cup grated Parmesan cheese

2 cups firmly packed fresh basil leaves

1/4 cup olive oil

Combine all the ingredients except the basil and olive oil in a food processor and process until smooth. Add the basil and olive oil and process for 15 to 20 seconds, until blended. Use the desired amount or spoon into muffin tins to freeze. Once frozen, the sauce can be stored in plastic freezer bags for up to 6 months.

BEEF, PORK & POULTRY

Plus the story of
Margaret Lupo, the
Queen of Greens and
owner of Mary Mac's
for 30 years

CLOCKWISE FROM TOP LEFT: MARGARET AND HARVEY LUPO; MARGARET LUPO AND FLO PATRICK, WHO WORKED WITH HER UNTIL 1992; LUPO AND HER DAUGHTER, MARIE LUPO NYGREN, AND HER THREE GRANDDAUGHTERS, AT SERENBE AFTER LUPO SOLD MARY MAC'S; LUPO WITH JOHN FER- RELL AT MARY MAC'S, AFTER SHE SOLD THE RESTAURANT TO HIM AND HELPED IN A CONSULTING CAPACITY.

MARGARET LUPO

MARGARET LUPO, the grande dame of classic Southern food in Atlanta, was the embodiment of Mary Mac's for over thirty years—from 1962 to 1994. Born Margaret Kennon in Salem, Alabama, in 1919, she grew up in Columbus, Georgia. She wisely followed her mother's advice and attended Georgia State College for Women in Milledgeville, earning a degree in Latin. At the age of nineteen, she graduated as valedictorian of her class. After college, Margaret moved back to Columbus and got married. By the time she arrived in Atlanta in the early 1950s, Margaret had already divorced, and was a single mother with a young son, Andrew. She and Andrew moved in with her sister, Merle, a nurse. In an age when most women didn't take jobs, Margaret had a child to support and not much choice in the matter. So she put her intelligence and ambition to work. For a time, she managed the food service department at the Luckie Street YMCA. She would later proudly point out that she "was the first person they ever hired that turned a profit." It was during this time that she became friends with other restaurant owners in the city, including Mary McKinsey.

Soon, Margaret opened her own small lunchtime restaurant, Margaret's Tray Shop, in downtown Atlanta. Most of her customers worked for a company called Retail Credit (now Equifax). When Retail Credit shut its office and moved, Margaret was forced to close her doors, too. She'd lost her first business but gained valuable restaurant experience for the future.

Life wasn't all hard knocks for Margaret, however. One welcome knock changed Margaret's life forever. Door-to-door salesman Harvey Lupo came calling at the house one morning in the late 1950s, and the two soon fell in love and got married. Harvey had three daughters from a previous marriage, Barbara, Judy, and Margaret. Margaret and Harvey later had two children of their own, Marie and Genie. As Margaret told the *Atlanta Journal* in 1985, "We never thought of the children as his or mine. I love them all the same, as did Harvey."

Margaret closed her downtown restaurant so that she could spend a few years at home

THE SKYLINE ROOM AT MARY MAC'S FROM THE 1980S

With one more expansion complete, another 100 seats were added, and Mary Mac's Tea Room now had room to seat 350 people.

"We were now a big restaurant even though we planned to stay a family-type Southern food tea room, still personally welcoming all our customers and friends," Margaret wrote of the move into the White Dot space (now the Skyline Room at Mary Mac's).

The most controversial expansion occurred in 1974. At the death of Fulton Pharmacy's owner, the storefront at the corner of Ponce de Leon Avenue and Myrtle Street became available. This space was too far from the kitchen to be a dining room. Instead, Margaret declared it would be the restaurant's main entrance, the reception room, and the bar. Buying a liquor license was highly unusual for a woman in the South in the 1970s, but Margaret plowed ahead with her usual determination. The mahogany pharmacist's counter was converted to the bar. "The biggest problem we had at first was in retraining the employees to ask each of

their customers if they cared for a drink from the bar. After the waitresses found that even that sweet little old lady replied with a 'Why, yes, thank you—a double martini on the rocks, please,' and that tips would increase, we had no more trouble," Margaret wrote. "For years customers could not really believe Mary Mac's sold liquor."

The Lupos went on to add other locations to create something of a Mary Mac's chain, including take-out stores and a Mary Mac's II. Harvey opened Mary Mac's II in the late 1960s in East Point, south of Atlanta. The location just wasn't right and after losing money for three years, it closed. For Margaret, the experience had a silver lining of sorts.

"It did make me sit down and write out all the recipes the cooks in the kitchen and I had been putting together for years, so it was not a complete loss," she remembered.

In 1977, much to Harvey's concern, Margaret built a take-out cafeteria in a corner of the restaurant's kitchen. Harvey was beginning to

LUPO OFTEN HELPED IN THE KITCHEN.

think Margaret would never settle down and be satisfied.

Margaret told the *Atlanta Journal*, "I nearly had to get a divorce when I decided to add the take-out business. Harvey was against it." The corner take-out room was about six steps lower than the level of the kitchen, with its own entrance to Myrtle Street, making it easy for customers to come directly in just for take-out. However, this also allowed food to easily "walk away" before it had been paid for, so the take-out area was eventually moved upstairs.

Three additional take-out locations, known as Mary Mac's To Go, were started when take-out orders grew to nearly 200 plates a day. The first location was opened on Roswell Road in January 1984. Soon to follow were locations on Peachtree Road and Edgewood Avenue. Most food for the take-out stores was cooked in the tea room's main kitchen and then driven to the take-out locations. Flora Hunter, a long-time cook, remembers working the night shift (11 p.m. to 7 a.m.) in order to make the food

that was to be delivered to the take-out locations in the morning. The take-out locations operated for a few years, but after not turning a significant profit, their doors were closed.

Meanwhile, Mary Mac's original location continued to thrive, with its reputation for classic Southern food spreading far beyond Atlanta. Mary Mac's was becoming a place for "destination dining." As Atlanta blossomed into the progressive capital of the New South, the city's famous visitors began to pop up at Mary Mac's looking for an authentic taste of Southern cuisine. Mary Mac's began to gain a reputation as a place where you could just as likely bump into a movie star or famous entertainer as you might an old friend.

It seems natural that a restaurant that serves a thousand diners a day would have plenty of parking spaces. Not so with Mary Mac's—not at first anyway. As the tea room's popularity grew, the 1980s brought one more expansion. As business along once-depressed Ponce de Leon Avenue stirred to life and picked up steam, Mary Mac's street-front parking became scarce. Margaret had no choice but to build a parking lot, and she did it with her own touch of style. She quietly purchased two houses located just behind the restaurant. Then, over the short space of a calm and sunny weekend, while the neighbors were thought to be busy with their activities, the two houses were flattened and hauled away, the lots were graded and smoothed, and a spacious new parking lot was paved. Needless to say, the surprised residents of Myrtle Street were less than enthusiastic about the newly paved lot. But with ample parking assured, Mary Mac's was ready to welcome the world.

FRIED CHICKEN

SERVES 4 TO 6

The secret to our fried chicken is the buttermilk.

1 (3-pound) fryer chicken, cut into serving pieces

2 teaspoons salt

1 teaspoon freshly ground black pepper

3/4 cup buttermilk

2 cups all-purpose flour

1/2 teaspoon white pepper

1 cup peanut oil

1/2 cup water

Rinse the chicken pieces and pat dry with paper towels. Sprinkle with 1 teaspoon of the salt and the 1 teaspoon of black pepper; let stand for 15 minutes. Place the buttermilk in a medium bowl. In another medium bowl, mix together the flour, the remaining 1 teaspoon salt, and the white pepper.

Heat the oil in a heavy 12-inch frying pan to 375°F. Dredge the chicken pieces, including the giblets, one at a time, in the buttermilk, then in the flour until well coated. Place the floured chicken pieces and giblets on a tray.

Place the large pieces of the chicken in the pan first; fit the smaller pieces around them, reserving the giblets. Cover, reduce the heat to medium, and brown all the pieces well on one side, 8 to 10 minutes. Turn the pieces over. Add the giblets; cover and cook until browned, 8 to 10 minutes. Uncover and add the water slowly and carefully to the chicken. Cover and steam for 5 minutes. Uncover and turn the pieces. Drain on paper towels. Serve on a warmed platter.

BAKED CHICKEN AND GRAVY

SERVES 4 TO 6

You can substitute boneless split chicken breasts if you prefer all-white meat.

1 (6- to 7-pound) whole roasting chicken	Freshly ground black pepper
4 cups water	1 tablespoon salted butter, melted
1 teaspoon salt, plus additional for seasoning the chicken	

Remove the neck and giblets from the chicken. In a medium saucepan, combine 2 cups of the water and the 1 teaspoon salt; add the neck and giblets. Bring to a simmer over medium heat and cook, covered, for 1 hour. Pour the liquid through a wire-mesh strainer into a bowl, reserving the solids, if using; set aside for the gravy. (The giblets may be chopped and reserved for the gravy.)

Preheat the oven to 325°F. Rinse the chicken and pat dry with paper towels. Sprinkle the skin and cavity of the chicken with salt and freshly ground pepper. Place the chicken in a Dutch oven and add the remaining 2 cups water to the bottom of the pan. Cover and bake for 1 1/2 hours, or until a meat thermometer inserted into the thickest part of the thigh without touching the bone registers 170°F.

Carefully tilt the pan and ladle out any remaining liquid, adding to the reserved giblet broth. Increase the oven temperature to 400°F. Brush the chicken with the melted butter and return to the oven. Bake for about 10 minutes, or until the top is golden brown. Transfer to a serving platter, reserving the pan drippings to make Baked Chicken Gravy.

BAKED CHICKEN GRAVY
(Makes about 2 cups)

2 cups giblet broth, reserved from above	Dash of hot sauce (optional)
3 tablespoons all-purpose flour	1/8 teaspoon freshly ground black pepper (optional)
1 cup whole milk	
1 cup water	1 tablespoon salted butter (optional)
1 teaspoon salt	Giblets, finely chopped (optional)
1/8 teaspoon white pepper	

Pour 1 1/2 cups of the broth into the same Dutch oven used to bake the chicken and heat to a simmer over medium heat. Scrape the browned bits from the sides and bottom of the Dutch oven.

In a small saucepan, heat the remaining 1/2 cup broth until warm. Whisk in the flour to form a smooth paste. Slowly add the flour mixture to the simmering broth in the Dutch oven, stirring to combine. Cook, stirring constantly, for about 5 minutes, or until the mixture is smooth and has thickened.

Combine the milk and water in a small bowl and slowly add the milk mixture to the gravy mixture, whisking until smooth. If the gravy is too thick, add more water or milk to reach the desired consistency. Add the salt and white pepper. Add the dash of hot sauce, the black pepper, and the 1 tablespoon butter. Add the giblets and serve with the baked chicken.

Favorite Diners

Photographers Arvel Crow and Billy Sherrill

Mary Mac's is not a chain restaurant, but two customers have taken our menu to international spots and recorded the images for us.

Arvel Crow was a longtime customer who has contributed globe-trotting images of the Mary Mac's menu to our files, including this one of London.

Billy Sherrill is another amateur photographer and customer who has added to the collection of images of Mary Mac's menus in exotic places.

He carried a menu with him when he visited Kuala Lumpur, Malaysia, in 1998; Abu Simbel in southern Egypt; and he snapped the photo, at right, of our menu in Sydney when he was working for the Olympics there.

Their photos hang on the walls at Mary Mac's, and serve to illustrate how "international" we have become!

CHICKEN AND SOUTHERN DUMPLINGS

SERVES 4 TO 6

I distinctly remember enjoying my first dish of chicken and dumplings at a dinner on the grounds of the Crawfordville First United Methodist Church.

I whole large chicken hen, cut into
   serving pieces
I tablespoon salted butter
I ¹/2 teaspoons salt
¹/2 teaspoon freshly ground black pepper

I large egg, lightly beaten
I tablespoon water
I teaspoon salted butter, melted
I cup all-purpose flour
¹/2 cup heavy cream

Place the chicken in a large pot and cover with water. Bring to a boil over medium-high heat. Reduce the heat to a simmer and cook for about I hour. Add the butter, I teaspoon of the salt, and the pepper.

Meanwhile, combine the egg, the I tablespoon water, the remaining ¹/2 teaspoon salt, and the melted butter in a bowl. Slowly add the flour, stirring until the mixture forms a ball. Wrap the dough in plastic wrap and chill for 30 minutes.

Turn the chilled dough onto a lightly floured surface and knead a few times. (Add additional flour to make the dough easy to handle.) Roll out to a ¹/8-inch thickness and cut into strips I by 4 inches long.

Bring the chicken to a boil over medium-high heat and slowly lower the strips of dough into the liquid. (Keeping the temperature at a boil will help prevent the dumplings from sticking together.) When all of the dumplings are in the pot, reduce the heat to a simmer and cook, covered, for about 30 minutes. Just before serving, stir in the heavy cream. Sprinkle with salt and pepper to taste.

CHICKEN WITH RICE

SERVES 4

8 tablespoons (1 stick) unsalted butter

1 (3-pound) chicken, cut into serving
  pieces

1 large yellow onion, chopped

1 cup diced celery

1 cup peeled, diced carrots

2 cups long-grain white rice

4 cups chicken broth

1 teaspoon salt

1/2 teaspoon freshly ground black pepper

Preheat the oven to 350°F. Melt the butter in a large, heavy skillet over medium-high heat and cook the chicken for about 4 minutes on each side, or until browned. Transfer the chicken to a plate or bowl. Reduce the heat to medium and sauté the onion, celery, and carrots until the onion is soft and translucent, about 5 minutes. Add the rice and stir to coat in the butter. Add the chicken broth; return the chicken and any juices to the pan. Add the salt and pepper. Let the chicken come to a boil over medium-high heat; cover with an ovenproof lid or foil and cook in the oven for 30 minutes, or until the chicken is cooked through and the rice is tender and the liquid is absorbed.

Favorite Diners

Judge Dorothy Beasley

Longtime customer Judge Dorothy Beasley has brought international guests to dine, such as former Romanian president Emil Constantinescu, who lunched with Judge Beasley during his visit to Atlanta in 1999. I made sure that Constantinescu tasted almost everything on the menu because Judge Beasley told me, "He needs a memorable local experience and this is the perfect place."

Judge Beasley once hosted the consul general of Belgium, Rita DeBruyne, for lunch. The two prominent women are still friends today. "Mary Mac's created an international friendship for me," Beasley recalls.

Appetizers

Fried Green Tomatoes served with a
parmesan horseradish dipping sauce..................$5.95

Fried Shrimp served with a cocktail sauce.............$7.25

Spicy Deep-Fried "Mudbugs", a heaping order
of Louisiana crawfish served with a
jalepeno tarter sauce $6.95

Lightly Fried Okra served with a
parmesan horseradish dipping sauce..................$4.?

Our lunch prices include hot breads.
No plate sharing, please.

BLUE PLATE SPECIAL - ASK YOUR S

Tearoom Favorites
SERVED WITH 2 SIDES

Fresh Vegetable Plate (choice of four side dishe

Baked Chicken with Cornbread Dressing & G

Country Fried Steak & Gravy......................

Fried Chicken (Three Legs or One Breast

Meatloaf with Tomato Sauce ....

Roast Pork with Dressing & Gravy ......

Chicken & Dumplings.............................

Baked Turkey with Dressing & Grav

Chicken Pot Pie ....

Pork Barbecue with Brunswick S

Smothered Chicken over Rice....

Extra Vegetable or Salad with F

Side

- Macaroni & Cheese
- French Fries
- Sweet Potato Soufflé
- Whipped Potatoes
- Baked Potato
- Vegetable Soup
- Creamed Corn
- Okra & Tomato
- Squash Soufflé
- Fried Green T
- Potato Cakes
- Steamed Ca
- Vegetable
- Fried Okr

- Applesa
- Cole Sla
- Green Sa
- Fresh Frui   2/09

*Salad Dressings: French, .
Honey Mustard, Oliv .

◔ Indicates one of our Vegetarian Frien

We are not responsible for lost or unattended articles.

Welcome to
MARY MAC'S
Tea Room

Serving Classic Southern Food
In The Heart of Atlanta
~ Since 1945 ~

Mary Mac's Tea Room
224 Ponce de Leon Avenue NE
Atlanta, Georgia 30308
(404) 876-1800
www.marymacs.com

PRIVATE PARTIES AND
OFF-SITE CATERING AVAILABLE

WEEKDAY LUNCH MENU

History

Back in 1945, Mary McKinsey opened Mary Mac's Tea Room. In those tough days right after the end of the World War, enterprising w a living, some of them mothers widowed by the war, were establishing restaurants all over Atlanta. Calling their establishments "tea ro was a polite way of elevating their endeavor. Though our restaurant has grown and changed over the years, it's still 1945 in the kitchen a We still do things the way Mary McKinsey, and her successor, renowned owner Margaret Lupo (1962 - 1994) did things. Every morning we bushels of corn, hand wash our carefully selected greens, and snap the fresh green beans by hand. We bake our own scrumptious breads an like old fashioned banana pudding and fresh Georgia peach cobbler, and brew up the best iced tea in the South. Today John Ferrell, Mrs. Lu hand-picked successor, carries on the tradition of serving his guests a genuine taste of the South. Our service is friendly and honest-to-good John and his staff treat each patron like a special guest invited home for dinner. Many personal touches go into the Mary Mac's experience...be ask for your complimentary cup of pot likker and cornbread if it's your first visit. Whether you're here with your family, or with a business, ch travel group, we guarantee you that the scents wafting out of our kitchen will tempt your taste buds and delight your senses. Welcome to Mary

Meeting Rooms • Banquet Facilities

Also Ava

$ 9.95

---

ask for your c
travel group, we guara

2/09

Welcome to
MARY MAC
Tea Roo

COUNTRY FRIED STEAK AND GRAVY

SERVES 4

Each year this dish always ranks in the top three customer favorites, based on the number of orders at Mary Mac's.

3/4 cup plus 3 tablespoons all-purpose flour

1 teaspoon salt

1/2 teaspoon plus 1/8 teaspoon freshly ground black pepper

4 (4-ounce) cube steaks

1/2 cup vegetable oil or 8 tablespoons (1 stick) unsalted butter

1 medium yellow onion, halved and cut into 1/4-inch slices

3 cups warm water

Mix the 3/4 cup of flour, 3/4 teaspoon of the salt, and the 1/2 teaspoon pepper in a bowl; dredge the cube steaks in the flour mixture, shaking gently to remove the excess flour. In a medium skillet, heat the vegetable oil or melt the butter over medium heat. Brown the steaks for 3 minutes on each side and transfer to a 13 by 9-inch baking dish, reserving the drippings in the skillet for the gravy.

Preheat the oven to 350°F. Return the same skillet to medium heat. Add the onion and cook until soft and translucent, 4 to 5 minutes. Add the 3 tablespoons flour, the remaining 1/4 teaspoon salt, and the 1/8 teaspoon pepper. Stir to coat the onion. Slowly add the water, whisking until smooth. Bring the gravy just to a boil and stir until thickened. Pour the gravy over the steaks in the baking dish and bake for 15 minutes. Serve the steaks in the gravy with steamed rice or whipped potatoes.

CHICKEN AND YANKEE DUMPLINGS

1 whole large chicken hen

2 teaspoons salt

1/2 teaspoon freshly ground black pepper

2 cups all-purpose flour

2 teaspoons baking powder

2 tablespoons cold salted butter, cut into small pieces

1 cup buttermilk

Place the chicken in a large pot and add water to cover; add 1 teaspoon of the salt. Bring to a boil over medium-high heat; reduce to a simmer and cook until tender, about 1 to 1 1/2 hours. Transfer the chicken to a shallow bowl, reserving the liquid in the pot. Let the chicken cool until you are able to pull the meat from the bones into bite-sized pieces. Discard the skin and bones and return the chicken to the pot. Add the pepper.

Meanwhile, combine the flour, baking powder, and the remaining 1 teaspoon salt. With a pastry blender or 2 forks, cut the pieces of cold butter into the flour mixture until the mixture resembles coarse cornmeal. Add the buttermilk and stir well until a soft dough forms.

Bring the pot of chicken to a boil, reduce the heat to a simmer, and drop the dough into the liquid in the pot by large spoonfuls. Simmer for about 10 minutes, or until the dough is puffed and cooked through.

MEATLOAF WITH TOMATO SAUCE

SERVES 4 TO 6

A very good, hearty meatloaf re-created in Mary Mac's kitchen by Flora Hunter for more than thirty-five years—and it is as popular as ever.

2 pounds ground beef

1 1/2 cups diced onion

1 cup diced green bell pepper

1 cup uncooked oatmeal

1/2 cup ketchup

2 tablespoons Worcestershire sauce

2 teaspoons Heinz 57 sauce

1/2 teaspoon white pepper

1/4 teaspoon salt

2 large eggs, lightly beaten

Tomato Sauce (recipe follows)

Preheat the oven to 350°F. Lightly grease a 9 by 5-inch loaf pan. Combine all the ingredients except the tomato sauce in a large bowl. Place the meat mixture in the loaf pan and bake for 55 minutes. Pour off the drippings and bake for 10 minutes longer to brown. Remove from the oven and pour the tomato sauce over the top to serve.

TOMATO SAUCE

(Makes about 1 cup sauce)

1 tablespoon salted butter

1 cup tomato sauce

1/4 cup firmly packed light brown sugar

1 teaspoon Worcestershire sauce

Melt the butter over medium-low heat in a small, heavy saucepan. Add the remaining ingredients and stir to combine. Cover and cook for about 10 minutes, stirring occasionally. Serve warm with the meatloaf.

BBQ RIBS

SERVES 6 TO 8

These ribs are fantastic to make ahead and freeze. Simply thaw and warm up for a last-minute meal or party fare.

1 tablespoon salt	2 full slabs St. Louis-style ribs
1 tablespoon freshly ground black pepper	2 cups water
1 tablespoon garlic powder	1 teaspoon liquid smoke

Preheat the oven to 350°F. Rub the salt, pepper, and garlic powder evenly over the ribs. Combine the water and liquid smoke in a roasting pan. Place the ribs, bone side down, in the pan and cover tightly with aluminum foil. Cook for 3 1/2 to 4 hours, until the ribs are tender enough to remove from the bone. Serve with barbecue sauce.

BARBECUE SAUCE
(Makes about 4 cups)

2 cups cider vinegar	2 teaspoons hot sauce
2 cups brown sugar	1/8 teaspoon crushed red pepper flakes
1 tablespoon salt	1/2 teaspoon freshly ground black pepper
1 tablespoon freshly squeezed lemon juice	1/8 teaspoon cayenne pepper
2 teaspoons soy sauce	

Combine all the ingredients in a large saucepan. Bring to a boil over medium-high heat; reduce the heat and simmer for 15 minutes. Let cool.

COUNTRY HAM WITH REDEYE GRAVY

SERVES 4

If you can't find country ham at your grocery store, buy it online from Keene's in Bardstown, Kentucky (keeneshams.com).

2 (8-ounce) country ham steaks
Vegetable oil
3/4 cup black coffee
3/4 cup water

Rinse the ham steaks and pat dry with paper towels. Cut off the brown rind around the ham slices, leaving the fat. In a large, heavy skillet, add the oil to barely coat the bottom of the pan. Heat the oil over medium heat. Brown the ham steaks for 3 minutes on each side; transfer the ham to a warm platter, reserving the drippings in the pan. Reduce the heat to low and add the coffee to the drippings in the pan. Add the water slowly and stir well, scraping the browned bits from the bottom of the pan. The gravy will be dark red and salty. Serve the ham with grits and biscuits to soak up the gravy.

Favorite Diners

Max Cleland, Former U.S. Senator

Politicians love Mary Mac's, not only for the food, but for its close proximity to the state capitol building, so we see a lot of them. Max Cleland is definitely one of our favorites. Being wheelchair-bound doesn't slow Max down; he has been a faithful customer for many years. When I asked him to lend a few words to this book about how he feels about Mary Mac's, his comment was, "Mary Mac's? It's my home. Period. Home cookin', home lovin', and hometown people!"

GRILLED LIVER AND ONIONS

SERVES 6 TO 8

You can't find grilled liver on many restaurant menus these days, but it has been a popular item at Mary Mac's for sixty-plus years.

2 tablespoons salted butter

2 large sweet onions, halved and cut into
   1/4-inch slices

8 tablespoons (1 stick) butter

8 (4-ounce) slices beef liver

Salt and freshly ground black pepper

Melt the 2 tablespoons butter in a large sauté pan over medium heat. Add the onions and sauté until soft and translucent, 4 to 5 minutes. Reduce the heat to low.

In another large sauté pan, melt the 8 tablespoons butter. Sauté the liver slices in batches for about 2 minutes on each side. Serve the liver with the sautéed onions.

INDIAN CAMP CHILI STEW

SERVES 16 TO 20

1 pound ground beef

1 pound ground sweet Italian sausage

1 pound lean ground turkey

3 medium sweet onions, diced

2 tablespoons olive oil

2 heads of garlic, cloves separated and peeled, then minced

3 (28-ounce) cans whole tomatoes, crushed by hand with the juices reserved

4 (16-ounce) cans dark red kidney beans, drained and rinsed

2 (14 1/2-ounce) cans diced tomatoes, undrained

2 (11-ounce) cans whole kernel corn, undrained

1 (10-ounce) can tomatoes with diced hot green peppers

1 (15-ounce) can tomato sauce

1 (6-ounce) can tomato paste

1 yellow bell pepper, diced

1 red bell pepper, diced

1 green bell pepper, diced

1 tablespoon chili powder

1 tablespoon dried basil

1 teaspoon salt

1 teaspoon freshly ground black pepper

1 teaspoon crushed red pepper flakes

1 teaspoon chipotle chili powder

1 teaspoon garlic powder

1 teaspoon Greek seasoning

2 cups water

2 (9-ounce) packages fresh spinach

Sour cream, for garnish

Grated Cheddar cheese, for garnish

In a large frying pan, combine the beef, sausage, and turkey with 1 cup of the diced onions. Cook over medium-high heat until the meat is browned and crumbly. Drain the liquid.

To a large stockpot, add the olive oil and garlic and cook over medium heat until the garlic is softened, 2 to 3 minutes. Add the crushed tomatoes and their juices. Add the remaining onions and mix well. Add the drained beef, sausage, and turkey mixture, and the remaining ingredients except the spinach and garnishes. Stir well and bring to a boil, then reduce the heat, cover, and simmer for at least 1 hour before serving. Adjust the seasonings to taste.

To serve, place a few leaves of fresh spinach in each bowl, ladle the chili over the spinach, and top with a dollop of sour cream and freshly grated Cheddar cheese.

ITALIAN TURKEY AND VEGETABLE MEATLOAF

SERVES 4 TO 6

We sometimes refer to this as a holiday meatloaf due to the brilliant colors of the green and red bell peppers. The vegetables give it a wonderful flavor and it's great to freeze.

1 pound ground sweet Italian sausage

1 pound lean ground turkey

1 cup uncooked oatmeal

1 green bell pepper, chopped

1 red bell pepper, chopped

1 (9-ounce) package fresh spinach, chopped

8 cloves garlic, crushed

1 medium sweet onion, diced

1/4 cup olive oil

1 large egg

1/4 teaspoon dried basil

1/4 teaspoon dried oregano

1/4 teaspoon Greek seasoning

1/2 teaspoon dried parsley

Salt and freshly ground black pepper

Tomato Sauce (recipe follows)

Preheat the oven to 350°F. Lightly grease a 13 by 9-inch baking dish. In a large bowl, combine all the ingredients, except the tomato sauce. Form into a loaf and place in the baking dish; bake for 1 hour. Remove from the oven and pour the tomato sauce over the meatloaf to serve.

TOMATO SAUCE

1 tablespoon salted butter

1 cup canned tomato sauce

1/4 cup firmly packed light brown sugar

1 teaspoon Worcestershire sauce

Melt the butter over medium-low heat in a small, heavy saucepan. Add the remaining ingredients and stir to combine. Cover and cook for about 10 minutes, stirring occasionally. Serve warm over Italian Turkey and Vegetable Meatloaf.

"I'm called the 'goodwill ambassador' for Mary Mac's. I give back rubs to customers to help them relax. They even made a T-shirt for me that said, 'I got my belly filled and my back rubbed at Mary Mac's.'"

—Jo Carter

OLD SOUTH CHICKEN PILAU

SERVES 6

My first recollection of this dish was watching my mother cook over an open fire in a cast-iron pot that held freshly butchered chickens with the eggs still in the chicken, which added incredible flavor.

3¹/₂ pounds stewing chicken, cut into serving pieces	1 medium sweet onion, chopped
2 ounces fatback (salt pork), diced	3 cups cooked white rice
1 teaspoon salt	Pinch of freshly ground black pepper
2 tablespoons salted butter	¹/₄ cup finely chopped fresh parsley

Rinse the chicken and place it in a stockpot. Add the fatback to the chicken, cover with cold water, and bring to a boil over medium-high heat. Reduce the heat and simmer, covered, for 1 ¹/₂ to 2 hours, until the chicken is tender. Add the salt after the chicken has cooked for 1 hour.

Remove the chicken to a shallow bowl, reserving the liquid in a separate bowl. Let the chicken stand until cool enough to handle; remove the meat from the bones in bite-sized pieces. Return the chicken to the pot.

In a medium saucepan, melt the butter over medium heat and sauté the onion until softened and translucent, 4 to 5 minutes. Add the onion to the stockpot. Stir in the rice and enough of the reserved chicken broth to moisten. Heat until hot, adding the pepper and additional salt, if desired. Sprinkle the chopped parsley over the top to serve.

ROAST PORK WITH FRUIT SAUCE

SERVES 4 TO 6

1 (3 1/2 - to 4 1/4-pound) boneless Boston
  butt pork shoulder, trimmed
Salt and freshly ground black pepper
1 teaspoon rubbed dried sage
1/4 cup olive oil
2 large sweet onions, halved and cut into
  1/4-inch slices

4 cups seedless black grapes
3 tablespoons firmly packed light brown
  sugar
3/4 cup balsamic vinegar
3 cups chicken broth

Preheat the oven to 325°F. Rub the pork with 1/2 teaspoon salt, 1/2 teaspoon of the pepper, and the sage. In a Dutch oven, heat 2 tablespoons of the olive oil over medium-high heat. Sear the pork in the oil on all sides until browned; transfer to a plate.

Add the remaining 2 tablespoons olive oil and reduce the heat to medium. Sauté the onions until soft and translucent, 4 to 5 minutes. Add the grapes and the brown sugar and stir for 1 minute. Add the vinegar; increase the heat to medium-high and cook for 4 minutes. Add the chicken broth and return the pork to the Dutch oven with any juices that have accumulated on the plate. Cover and place in the oven; cook for 1 1/2 to 2 hours, until the pork is tender.

Transfer the pork to a serving plate, reserving the liquid in the Dutch oven. Bring the reserved liquid in the Dutch oven to a boil over medium-high heat, stirring until thickened, 5 to 6 minutes. Add salt and pepper to taste. Serve the sauce with the pork.

ROAST TURKEY BREAST

SERVES 10 TO 12

No need to wait for Thanksgiving for this treat. It is a quick, no-hassle way to roast turkey.

1 (9- to 10-pound) turkey breast
1 teaspoon salt
1 teaspoon pepper
2 tablespoons canola oil

Preheat the oven to 350°F. Cut the turkey breast in half crosswise. Rub the seasoning and oil over the turkey breast; place in a roasting pan with the cut sides down. Roast for 1 hour, or until the internal temperature reaches 165°F on a meat thermometer. Let the turkey stand, covered with aluminum foil, for 20 minutes before slicing, so the juices don't run out. Slice to serve.

THE WRITE STUFF

Some traditions at Mary Mac's are kept for sentimental reasons; some are maintained because they work so well. Having a jar of sharpened pencils on each table alongside the order forms is one habit that works too well to quit.

We keep pencils on the tables for filling out orders, a practice that Mary McKinsey had started. This way, if an order was incorrect, it would not be the server's fault. In the era before sophisticated computers, individually written orders were also an easy way to keep track of how many customers ate at Mary Mac's each day. These days we use computers to track sales, but the pencils stay.

GARLIC AND SCALLIONS PORK ROAST

SERVES 4 TO 6

Jo Carter, our "goodwill ambassador at Mary Mac's" provided this recipe, and it is, as they say in the South, "Uhmmmm, good!"

I (3 1/2- to 4 1/4-pound) boneless Boston butt pork shoulder, trimmed

4 cloves garlic, sliced

I teaspoon salt

I teaspoon freshly ground black pepper

1/4 cup olive oil

2 large sweet onions, cut into 1/4-inch-thick rings

1/2 teaspoon sugar (optional)

I cup water

I cup chopped scallions

Preheat the oven to 325°F. Using a small knife, cut slits into the pork and insert a slice of garlic into each slit. Rub the pork with 1/2 teaspoon of the salt and 1/2 teaspoon of the pepper. Heat 2 tablespoons of the olive oil in a Dutch oven over medium-high heat; brown the pork on all sides. Transfer to a plate.

Heat the remaining 2 tablespoons olive oil in the same pan and add the sliced onions, the remaining 1/2 teaspoon salt, and the remaining 1/2 teaspoon pepper. Add the sugar and sauté over medium heat until the onions are softened and translucent, 4 to 5 minutes. Return the pork and any juices to the pan. Add the I cup water. Cover tightly and place the pan in the oven. Braise for I 1/2 to I 3/4 hours, until the pork is tender. Transfer the pork to a carving board and cut into 1/4-inch-thick slices for serving. Add the scallions to the pan and stir until wilted. Spoon the scallion mixture over the pork to serve.

HAM AND YANKEE DUMPLINGS

SERVES 4 TO 6

I had this at a restaurant while traveling through Maryland and was so impressed that I came up with my own version of it for Mary Mac's.

I large leftover ham bone with some meat	2 teaspoons baking powder
8 cups water	2 tablespoons cold butter, cut into small
Salt and freshly ground black pepper	pieces
2 cups all-purpose flour	I cup buttermilk
I teaspoon salt	

In a saucepan, bring the ham bone and the water to a boil, then reduce the heat and simmer for 20 minutes. Add salt and pepper to taste.

To make the dumplings, combine the flour, I teaspoon salt, and baking powder in a medium bowl. Cut in the butter with your fingers or 2 forks until the mixture resembles coarse cornmeal. Add the buttermilk and stir until just combined.

With the broth still simmering, drop the dumpling dough into the pan by large spoonfuls. Simmer for about 10 minutes, or until the dough is puffed and cooked through.

Favorite Diners

Atlanta's Favorite Twins, Ruth and Ruby Crawford

One of the best things about running Mary Mac's is the people you see on a regular basis, those customers and friends who become part of the restaurant's history and "family." Sisters Ruth and Ruby Crawford served as Mary Mac's hostesses during the latter part of the 1990s, and, after retiring, would return to eat at Mary Mac's almost daily. Always dressed identically, they became locally known as Atlanta's most famous twins.

HONEY-GLAZED HAM WITH RAISIN SAUCE

SERVES 10 TO 12

This is a classic Southern ham, perfect for holiday feasts. Note the cola in the sauce!

1 (5-pound) ham, fully cooked
8 tablespoons (1 stick) salted butter
1/4 cup firmly packed brown sugar
1/4 cup freshly squeezed orange juice
2 cups honey

1 (15 1/4-ounce) can sliced pineapple rings
Whole cloves
Raisin Sauce (recipe follows)

Preheat the oven to 300°F. Line a 13 by 9-inch baking dish with aluminum foil. Place the ham in the baking dish. In a small saucepan, melt the butter; add the brown sugar, orange juice, and honey, stirring often, to make the glaze. Brush the glaze over the ham with a pastry brush. Keep the remaining glaze warm over very low heat. Place the ham in the oven and cook for 2 1/2 hours, basting with the glaze every 30 minutes.

Remove the ham from the oven and place the pineapple rings over the surface, inserting 1 whole clove into the center of each ring. Brush any remaining glaze over the pineapple and return the ham to the oven for 30 minutes. Let the ham stand for 20 minutes before slicing. Slice the ham to serve and top with the raisin sauce.

RAISIN SAUCE

2 tablespoons firmly packed brown sugar
1 teaspoon Dijon or yellow mustard
1 1/2 tablespoons cornstarch
1 cup freshly squeezed orange juice

1/3 cup raisins
1 tablespoon unsalted butter
1/2 cup cola

In a small saucepan, combine the brown sugar, mustard, cornstarch, and orange juice. Bring to a boil, then reduce the heat and continue to simmer until the mixture thickens, 6 to 8 minutes. Add the raisins and butter and cook for 3 to 4 minutes. Stir in the cola. Serve warm with the sliced ham.

BREAD & BEVERAGES

❧ ◆ ❧

Mary Mac's gets

a new owner

for a new millennium

❧ ◆ ❧

CLOCKWISE FROM TOP LEFT: MY OPENING DAY IN 1994; WE REFURBISHED THE DINING ROOMS AND PUT A CLEAN FACE ON MARY MAC'S WITHOUT CHANGING THE BASICS. MARGARET LUPO WITH ME DURING THE FIRST FEW MONTHS OF THE REOPENING; I MADE SURE THE MENU REMAINED FAITHFUL TO TRADITIONS. MY MOTHER PLAYED A BIG PART IN HELPING WITH THE OPENING AND PROVIDING ENCOURAGEMENT.

NEW OWNERS

OVER TIME, Margaret Lupo's sure hands and good business sense fashioned Mary Mac's into the Southern landmark it is today. She created a place that felt like home to thousands of customers, many of them newcomers to the growing city. Margaret arrived most mornings by 7 a.m. and worked like a dynamo all day. By 11:15 in the morning, Tiger, the bartender, would be sitting at a table, stringing fresh green beans. Prepping fresh vegetables requires a large amount of time, so it was never unusual for every spare hand to chip in to get the work done. Harvey would be behind the cash register with a handful of gardenias he picked from the Lupos' garden that morning. Margaret would just have finished her morning taste-testing and would be darting around from room to room, checking all corners of the tea room, ensuring that all was ready for the upcoming lunch rush. The daily menus would be out and ready, stamped with the specials of the day. Then, as now, the tea room was a bustling place, and Margaret knew every aspect of her business.

She could be found behind the cash register, out in the dining rooms greeting customers and clearing tables, or in the kitchen calling orders during the busy lunchtime hour. Managing the kitchen staff wasn't an easy task in the beginning. When she bought the tea room, Margaret was young compared to most of the cooks in the kitchen. A resourceful woman, Margaret found a way to earn respect from her new employees. One by one, the cooks went on vacation. While they were gone, Margaret made sure she took each of their places instead of hiring a temporary replacement. Not only did she cook just as wonderfully and efficiently as the absent employee, but she also left that particular station much cleaner than she found it. At the return of the well-rested cook, a new bond of respect was formed. For many, this respect often grew into a strong friendship between Margaret and her employees. On Friday nights, she encouraged the employees to take any left-over food home to their own families.

With hard work and a sure business sense, Margaret steadily turned her tea room into a mecca for Southern dining. Then, early one morning in February 1982, the phone at the tea room rang. Harvey had died. Mary Mac's and the Lupo home changed in an instant. Margaret wrote, "Most of the fun went out for me. I still enjoyed the tea room, but it was never really the same."

It was the end of an era for Lupo and Mary Mac's. As the 1990s opened, chronic leg pain and her age brought Margaret to the tough realization that she should think about retiring. She loved the business dearly, but the demanding fifteen-hour days were simply too taxing for her. The summer of 1991 brought an announcement that Atlanta never expected to hear—Mary Mac's was for sale.

More than a year passed before she had a buyer for the successful restaurant. Stephen Choi became the unlikely new owner of the Atlanta landmark. Mr. Choi, a native of Korea, left his life as a restaurateur in Los Angeles to bring his wife and son to Atlanta to take charge of Mary Mac's Tea Room. Choi bought the business and the equipment, but Lupo remained the owner of the land beneath it.

"I'll still be landlady, and I'll still be associated with the business as a consultant," she told the *Atlanta Journal-Constitution* when news of the sale was announced.

One short month later, for reasons not entirely known, Choi put Mary Mac's back on the market, looking for a new owner. After being unsuccessful in moving his family to Atlanta, Choi sold the restaurant to a purchaser who would forever change the history of the tea room.

Lee Effenson bought Mary Mac's in December of 1992. By January, the tea room was up and running again—and even thriving. But 1993 unfolded as a year of unsteady growth, legal

troubles, and the eventual closing of Mary Mac's doors.

Effenson was new to the restaurant business, but had been involved with his family's liquor store chain in Florida before coming to Atlanta. He began his stint as Mary Mac's owner with an energetic vision for expanding the business while ensuring the Lupos' standards continued to be met. In the first few months of operation, Effenson hired some previous staff who had left while Choi was the owner. He brought back some of Margaret's recipes that had been shelved during Choi's brief ownership.

To the business community, Mary Mac's appeared to be flourishing and growing under its new owner. In June, Effenson announced plans to open four new Mary Mac's locations. The first location opened on Hugh Howell Road in Tucker, and a Cheshire Bridge location opened shortly thereafter. He also planned for a downtown location and one at Cumberland Mall (neither of which opened). Effenson told the *Atlanta Journal* that he planned to open six more locations within the following twelve months.

In anticipation of the ambitious expansion, he instructed veteran staff members to train new employees to work at the new locations. Each location was to serve breakfast in addition to lunch and dinner, with all having full-service bars. He told his staff, "If we put blindfolds on our customers, they shouldn't be able to tell which Mary Mac's they're in."

In August, Effenson announced the grand encore to his previous expansions would be a 4,400-square-foot location at Underground Atlanta. A November opening was planned. By mid-September, his plans, as well as his financial situation, were crumbling around him. After three criminal warrants were issued for his arrest in Florida, his reign at Mary Mac's careened to a dramatic close. Plans for the Underground Atlanta location were canceled, and Margaret began to receive calls from creditors about unpaid bills, as even more allegations surfaced out of Florida. While Margaret feared that her good name might be muddied, Effenson said, "I feel like Hank Aaron, who said the worst year of his life was the year he broke Babe Ruth's record. Ms. Lupo is Babe Ruth and I'm Hank Aaron." Effenson continued to deny the allegations as they surfaced.

After three months of swirling problems and uncertainty, Effenson closed all Mary Mac's locations, including the original tea room, and moved out of the city of Atlanta.

Margaret told the newspaper that almost $100,000 in unpaid bills existed, and ten of Lee's tea room employees had not been paid in three weeks. The doors were locked, the electricity was cut off due to lack of payment, and filth covered the kitchens. Any food that remained in the freezers and refrigerators was left to rot.

At this low point, it seemed that the venerable restaurant would live on only in memories. Margaret was brokenhearted at what seemed a horrible end to the business she had so lovingly and diligently built.

I entered Mary Mac's world at a time when it was filled with debt and turmoil and seemed lost beyond saving. However, I had a dream of owning a restaurant that served good-quality Southern food.

I had learned the love of Southern food and culture at a very young age, growing up in Florida. As a child, I learned how to grow

At this low point, it seemed that the venerable restaurant would live on only in memories. Margaret was brokenhearted at what seemed a horrible end to the business she had so lovingly and diligently built.

vegetables. My dad suffered two heart attacks when I was seven years old. I learned to cook at this young age to help my mother care for my father, who later recovered completely.

I grew up on the same food that we serve at Mary Mac's. We didn't have yeast rolls, but we had cornbread. My dad made great cornbread. We lived on a large farm in Wakulla County, Florida, and I often spent summers in Pensacola, helping my grandparents with their two motels. I assisted weary travelers with their bags and quickly learned that I loved the business of hospitality. I even enjoyed getting a dime tip when I took our guests' luggage to their rooms!

I was inspired to major in hotel and restaurant management at Florida State University. A friendship I developed in college would ultimately change my life—I'd met Marie Lupo, Margaret and Harvey Lupo's daughter.

As a member of the Society of Hosts, an organization at Florida State that visits restaurants for tours and a meal, I ate at Mary Mac's for the first time in the late 1970s. The Lupos offered the tea room as a destination for the group. We enjoyed breakfast and toured the massive kitchen after eating. I was amazed at the enormous kitchen. Up until that point, I had never seen one so large and efficient. Little did I know that one day I would be the master of that kitchen.

After college, I moved to Atlanta and dabbled in a variety of careers. I veered away from hospitality to enter the real estate business. Longing to be a part of the restaurant business, I moved to Cashiers, North Carolina, and managed a restaurant for a year, then returned to Atlanta and once again was back in real estate.

Around Thanksgiving in 1993, I took a fateful jog around midtown and spotted a "For Lease" sign hanging on Mary Mac's front door. I made a phone call to my friend Marie Lupo, Margaret's daughter, who filled me in on the long list of troubles at Mary Mac's. She didn't try to talk me out of it, though. In fact, Marie encouraged me to give her mother a call, and my dream to own this landmark restaurant began to take shape.

Marie Lupo Nygren and her husband, Steve, co-founder of the Pleasant Peasant restaurant chain, and also a dear friend of mine, were instrumental in encouraging me to reopen the restaurant.

Margaret and I struck a deal allowing me to lease the restaurant with an option to buy the property. As the Mary Mac's brochure says, "Margaret handpicked John both for his ability and his passion for good food and ipeccable service." Many days of cleaning, restoration, and repair work were needed before Mary Mac's could reopen. My parents and friends worked through December and into January 1994 to renovate, scrub, and remodel the entire building.

My dad, John Ferrell Sr., told me I was crazy when he first saw the place. "I said for him to run like hell," my father used to tell people. "That was the nastiest restaurant I had ever seen." That all changed with a few coats of paint, lots of soap, and new carpets. I wasn't scared of the responsibility, plus I felt like I could make it work. And Margaret promised to give me her invaluable support.

. . . I took a fateful jog around midtown and spotted a "For Lease" sign hanging on Mary Mac's front door. I made a phone call to my friend Marie Lupo, Margaret's daughter, who filled me in on the long list of troubles at Mary Mac's. She didn't try to talk me out of it, though.

Over two months of work came to a celebratory climax on February 2, 1994, when the doors at 224 Ponce de Leon opened for the first time since November. I put new tablecloths on all the tables and changed out worn old plates for new white china. I bought new silverware, but most importantly, I left the recipes and the service alone. I even rehired several longtime employees who had left when Effenson took over the restaurant. Mary Brown, Flora Hunter, and Flo Patrick all came back when they learned that the new owner was restoring the tea room directly under the supervision of Margaret "Mother" Lupo.

Margaret stood beside me every day for those first six months of 1994. She taught me her method of tasting and seasoning dishes, including her opinion that "pot likker is very hard to get seasoned right." I wanted to learn everything Margaret could teach me about the restaurant, and told her to treat me like her student. I tried to learn all I could from her about the business that she had devoted so much of her life to.

After things got rolling for me, Margaret continued to "consult" at the restaurant for a few days each week, unpaid, until January 1997. She enjoyed lending her advice and experience and taking a walk around the dining rooms to greet old friends with her trademark motherly rub on the back. By that January, I had reached the glorious point of exercising my right to buy the property. Mary Mac's Tea Room was officially and finally mine.

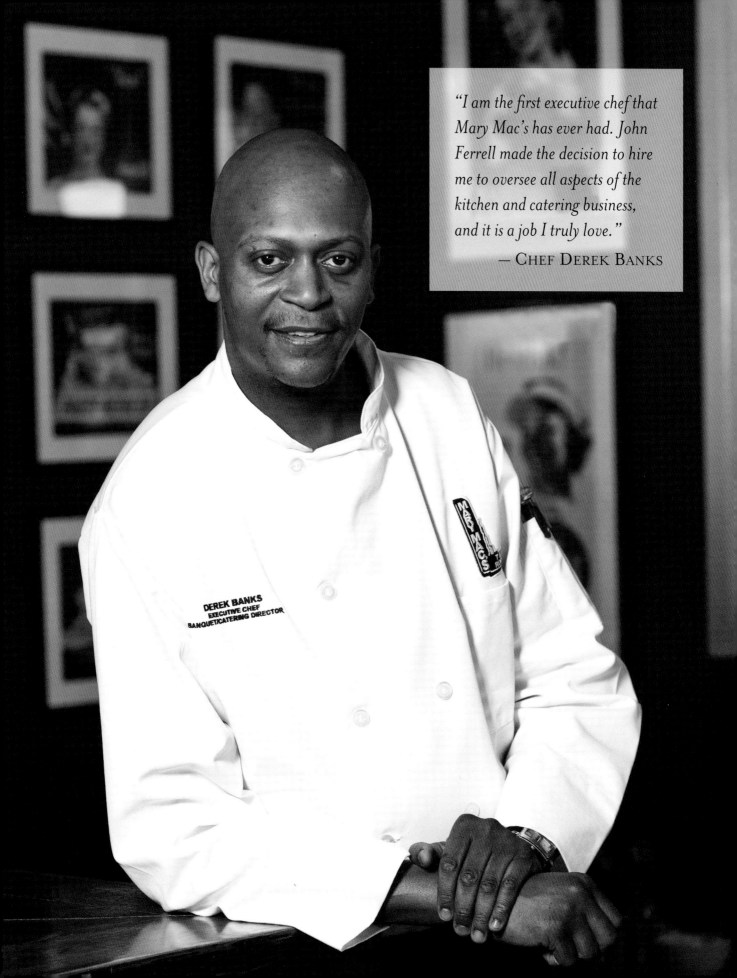

"I am the first executive chef that Mary Mac's has ever had. John Ferrell made the decision to hire me to oversee all aspects of the kitchen and catering business, and it is a job I truly love."

— CHEF DEREK BANKS

CINNAMON ROLLS

MAKES ABOUT A DOZEN ROLLS

YEAST DOUGH

1 package active dry yeast

1/2 teaspoon plus 1 tablespoon sugar

1/2 cup warm (100° to 110°F) water

4 cups all-purpose flour

1 teaspoon salt

1 large egg, lightly beaten

5 tablespoons vegetable shortening, melted

1 (5-ounce) can evaporated milk, warmed

Lightly oil a large bowl and set aside.

To make the dough, in the work bowl of a stand mixer, combine the yeast, the 1/2 teaspoon sugar, and the warm water and let stand for 5 minutes, or until bubbly. With the dough hook attachment on low speed, mix together the flour, the 1 tablespoon sugar, the salt, egg, shortening, and the evaporated milk. Add the yeast mixture to the flour mixture and continue to mix for about 5 minutes. Alternatively, you may knead the dough by hand on a floured surface for 10 minutes. The dough will be shiny, smooth, and sticky. Turn out into the oiled bowl, cover with a damp kitchen towel or plastic wrap, and let rise in a warm (85°F) place for 1 1/2 hours, or until doubled.

Punch the dough down, return to the bowl, cover, and let rise again for 1 hour, or until doubled. Punch the dough down once more, then pat the dough into a 12 by 8-inch rectangle.

Preheat the oven to 400°F. Grease a baking sheet with butter and set aside.

FILLING

12 tablespoons (1 1/2 stick) salted butter, softened

3/4 cup sugar

1 1/2 teaspoons ground cinnamon

To make the filling, in a small bowl, mix together the butter, sugar, and cinnamon until smooth. Reserve about 2 tablespoons. Using a spatula, spread the remaining filling over the surface of the dough to the edges. Working from the short side, roll up the dough into a log. Cut the roll into 1-inch pieces and place on the baking sheet with the sides touching. Sprinkle the reserved filling over the top.

Let the rolls rise for about 20 minutes in a warm place. Place in the oven and bake for about 25 minutes, or until the tops are golden brown. If the rolls rise while baking, gently pat them down, using a spatula.

"I've been here for fifteen years. I can make anything you want to drink, but my specialty is margaritas."

—WILLIAM JOHNSON

MARTINIS AT MARY MAC'S

Monsignor Donovan and I first started meeting for lunch in the mid-'70s when I moved to Atlanta after graduating from college. His parish was in Decatur and I would drive over to the parish house and join him for a lunch of fried chicken prepared by the rectory's wonderful cook. Before lunch he would mix us a martini in his study, and a tradition was started. Eventually he was transferred to a parish in Cumming, Georgia, which was a good distance from my office and, to make matters worse, there were no martinis to be had in the entire county. We still had lunch on occasion, but the distance and the lack of restaurants put our tradition on a temporary (seven-year) hiatus. In 1988 the Church transferred him to the Sacred Heart parish in downtown Atlanta. What a blessing!

It didn't take us long to start meeting for lunch once a week and having our martinis. Our dining experience at Mary Mac's was rewarding, but there was one drawback that kept us from attending on a regular basis and that was that no one could prepare a decent martini. We even resorted to mixing our own martinis after a waitress, exasperated, gave up trying to meet our standards. Another hindrance was the absence of martini glasses at Mary Mac's. Drinking martinis from wineglasses is akin to eating filet mignon from a paper plate. Regardless, we started to come in for lunch on a regular basis, because we realized that we could enjoy two martinis at Mary Mac's for what we paid for one at a fancier place—and still have an excellent meal! That decision fixed our lunch destination for the next eighteen years.

Next, we had to resolve the dilemma of the absence of martini glasses, and find someone at Mary Mac's who could properly mix the drinks. One day we had the good fortune to be sitting at William Johnson's table (he has since become an essential part of our tradition at Mary Mac's). When we placed our usual order of "two martinis, extra dry, up with a twist" (vodka and shaken), William, without any hesitation, took the order and filled it to perfection. William not only could mix the perfect martini, but he had procured two martini glasses, too.

We became such regular patrons that Jo Carter, the "goodwill ambassador," announced to the entire dining room whenever we entered that the "tuni guys" are here. Everything was going along splendidly until one day at lunch we suffered a great misfortune. After we finished our lunch and martinis, Monsignor rose from his chair and leaned on the edge of the table for support. As fate would have it, the table toppled over and every dish and glass crashed to the floor. After I was sure that the Monsignor was all right, I frantically searched through the pile of dishes for the martini glasses. Not a dish or water glass was broken, but the two martini glasses were smashed, scattered across the floor in hundreds of shards. William assured us not to worry, that the manager would be notified and he would immediately place an order for a case of martini glasses.

The tradition continues to this day. We still make our martini visits, mostly on Tuesdays or Wednesdays. Three years ago the Monsignor moved into a retirement village in Roswell, about twenty miles away. He is now ninety-four years old and has indicated to me that the highlight of his week is his visit to Mary Mac's for martinis and lunch. I told him I feel the same way and the only thing that could upset our scheduled visit would be a shortage of martini glasses, but that would be only temporary because I know William has two backups hidden somewhere.

I'll have another one straight up and pass the chicken, please.

—TONY TOTIS,
customer for almost two decades

BUTTERMILK BISCUITS

MAKES 10 TO 12 BISCUITS

2 cups self-rising flour

1 1/2 teaspoons baking powder

1/8 teaspoon salt

1/2 teaspoon cream of tartar

1 tablespoon sugar

1/4 cup vegetable shortening

3/4 cup buttermilk

Preheat the oven to 400°F. Grease a baking sheet. In a large bowl, mix together the dry ingredients. Cut in the shortening with your fingers or 2 forks until the mixture resembles coarse cornmeal. Add the buttermilk and mix lightly. Turn out the dough onto a lightly floured board and roll to a 3/4-inch thickness. Add as little extra flour as possible. Cut the dough with a 3-inch round biscuit or cookie cutter and place on the baking sheet. Bake for 10 to 12 minutes, until the bottoms are lightly browned.

OUR TAXI SERVICE

We call a lot of taxis to pick up visitors who are staying at downtown hotels. But like all large cities, at some times of night and in some weather it's just not easy to get a taxi. My partner, Hank Thompson, tells this story about one such incident.

"Late one rainy night as John was leaving Mary Mac's, he noticed a man standing inside the lobby asking the hostess to call a cab for him. John approached and asked if everything was all right, to which the man replied, 'Yes, I just had a marvelous meal and I am waiting for a cab to get back to my downtown hotel.'

John offered, 'Just come on and ride with me; I will be happy to drop you off.'

The man accepted and during the ride and the conversation, John told him he was the owner of Mary Mac's.

The man remarked, 'My! This is what I call Southern hospitality!'

A year passed and one night John noticed a middle-aged couple standing outside Mary Mac's, and asked them if they needed any help. They replied that they were here from up north and were simply waiting for a cab to take them back to a downtown hotel.

Of course, John offered this couple a ride with him and they accepted. In the car, they both began to laugh and John asked them what was so funny.

'Well,' they replied, 'our dentist back home told us about this marvelous Southern restaurant where he had dined last year, and that the owner even gave him a ride home afterward—but we didn't believe him. But now, we clearly see he wasn't kidding!'"

HUSH PUPPIES

MAKES 24 TO 30 HUSH PUPPIES

1 cup white cornmeal

1 teaspoon baking powder

1 teaspoon salt

1 tablespoon sugar

1/4 teaspoon baking soda

1/2 teaspoon freshly ground black pepper

3 tablespoons all-purpose flour

1 medium sweet onion, finely chopped

3/4 cup buttermilk

1 large egg

4 cups vegetable oil

Combine the dry ingredients in a large, shallow mixing bowl. Stir the onion into the dry ingredients. Whisk together the buttermilk and egg in a separate bowl; add to the dry ingredients and mix well. Add 1 tablespoon of the vegetable oil to the batter. Spread a small amount of oil over the batter in the bowl. Reserve the rest of the oil for frying.

Heat the remaining oil in a large cast-iron skillet over medium-high heat. Using a clean spoon, scoop out 1/2 tablespoon–sized balls and drop them immediately into the hot oil. Clean and re-oil the spoon each time you add more balls to the oil, so the batter doesn't stick to the spoon. The hush puppies should roll over in the oil by themselves, but if not, you may need to turn them once. Cook for 3 to 4 minutes, until the bottoms are golden brown, turning once and frying until the hush puppies are golden brown, crunchy, and floating to the top. Place on paper towels to drain. Serve hot.

JOHN FERRELL'S CORNBREAD

SERVES 8 TO 10

Although I like to make skillet cornbread at home, this recipe works for corn muffins, too, which is what we serve in the restaurant.

1/4 cup corn oil or bacon drippings plus 2 tablespoons for the skillet	1 teaspoon salt
1 1/2 cups white cornmeal plus 1 tablespoon for the skillet	1 1/2 teaspoons baking powder
	1/2 teaspoon baking soda
1/4 cup self-rising flour	1 cup buttermilk
1 tablespoon sugar	1 large egg

Preheat the oven to 450°F. Grease a 10-inch cast-iron skillet with 2 tablespoons corn oil or bacon drippings and place it in the oven for 6 to 8 minutes, until very hot. Combine the 1 1/2 cups white cornmeal, the flour, sugar, salt, baking powder, and baking soda in a large bowl. Mix together the buttermilk, the remaining 1/4 cup oil or drippings, and egg in a small bowl. While the skillet is in the oven, stir the wet ingredients into the dry until just combined. Do not overstir. Remove the hot skillet from the oven and sprinkle the 1 tablespoon cornmeal evenly over the bottom. This prevents the cornbread from sticking. Immediately pour the batter into the skillet and return to the oven. Bake for 18 to 20 minutes, or until browning on the edges. Serve hot.

VARIATION: Alternatively, the batter can be poured into a well-greased muffin tin to make about a dozen cornbread muffins.

GRANDDADDY FERRELL'S EGGNOG

SERVES 4

This was my grandfather's holiday recipe served only to his special guests and friends, and always accompanied by Mama's pound cake. When we asked him if the raw eggs in the recipe were bad for him, he replied, "Hell, no, the whiskey cooks them!"

4 large eggs, separated
1/4 cup sugar
4 jiggers whiskey
Sprinkle of ground nutmeg

Using a hand mixer, beat the egg yolks and sugar together in a small bowl; add the whiskey (the whiskey "cooks" the yolks). In a medium bowl, with clean beaters free of yolk, whip the egg whites until light peaks form. Fold the yolk mixture into the whipped egg whites. Pour into 4 glasses and sprinkle with nutmeg to serve.

NOTE: *This recipe contains uncooked egg. This may be a health concern for the very young, the elderly, pregnant women, and those with weak immune systems.*

"SWEET TEA, PLEASE!"

Legions of ice tea pitchers stand ready for thirsty customers throughout the day and evening at Mary Mac's. Although a few transplants to Atlanta request unsweet, by far the favorite is our sweet tea. *Travel and Leisure* magazine gave a shout-out to Mary Mac's in a review from their April 2003 issue, writing, "Call your dentist: the iced tea here is the epitome of Southern sweet."

Lattes and green teas may come and go, but we Southerners know that a cool glass of sweet tea is the perfect drink in the scalding heat of our Atlanta summers.

We like to refer to it as "the table wine of the South."

HOLIDAY EGGNOG

SERVES 20

This was a favorite of my aunt Mavis Young of Leesburg, Florida.

6 large eggs, separated

1 cup sugar

1 1/2 cups Christian Brothers brandy

1/2 cup light rum

6 cups whole milk

3 cups whipping cream

Ground or freshly grated nutmeg

Whisk the egg yolks until thick and light. Add the sugar slowly, continuing to whisk constantly. Gradually add the brandy and rum, whisking constantly. Chill for 1 hour.

Stir the milk into the alcohol mixture slowly. In the work bowl of a stand mixer with the whisk attachment, on medium-high speed, beat the egg whites and whipping cream until stiff. Fold the beaten egg whites and whipped cream into the alcohol mixture. Store in covered jars in the regrigertor for at least a day if possible before serving. Sprinkle each serving with nutmeg. Stir the eggnog in the punch bowl as you serve it, otherwise you will get too much fluff on one serving and not enough on the next.

NOTE: *This recipe contains uncooked egg. This may be a health concern for the very young, the elderly, pregnant women, and those with weak immune systems.*

PEACH BUTTERMILK PANCAKES

SERVES 4 TO 6

2 1/2 cups all-purpose flour

2 tablespoons sugar

2 teaspoons baking powder

1 teaspoon baking soda

1/2 teaspoon ground cinnamon

1/8 teaspoon salt

2 large eggs

1 1/2 cups buttermilk

2 tablespoons unsalted butter, melted

1 1/2 cups canned peach chunks, drained
(may substitute diced fresh peaches or
whole fresh berries)

Maple syrup

Sift together the flour, sugar, baking powder, baking soda, cinnamon, and salt into a large bowl. In a medium bowl, beat the eggs with a whisk until well blended; add the buttermilk and beat well. Add the egg mixture to the dry ingredients and mix until just combined. Gently stir in the melted butter and the peaches.

Lightly butter a large, heavy skillet or griddle and place over medium heat. Pour about 1/3 cup of batter into the skillet for each pancake, making 2 or 3 at a time. (Do not over-crowd the skillet.) Cook the pancakes, in batches, for 3 to 4 minutes, until the tops are covered with bubbles and the edges look cooked; turn with a spatula and cook until the bottoms are browned and the centers are cooked through. Repeat with the remaining batter, adding more butter to the skillet as needed. Serve with warm maple syrup.

ICE CREAM–BLUEBERRY MUFFINS

MAKES 6 MUFFINS

A sweet way to remember summer days and ice cream cones on a cold winter morning.

1 cup vanilla ice cream, softened

1 cup self-rising flour

1 cup fresh blueberries

1 tablespoon salted butter, melted

2 tablespoons sugar

Preheat the oven to 375°F. Grease a 6-cup muffin tin. In a medium bowl, mix the ice cream and flour together well. Fold in the blueberries and spoon into the muffin cups. Bake for 20 to 25 minutes, until a wooden toothpick inserted into the center of a muffin comes out clean. While hot, brush the muffin tops with the butter and sprinkle with the sugar. Remove from the pan immediately. Serve warm.

MS. LIL'S SPOON BREAD

SERVES 6 TO 8

2/3 cup white cornmeal

1 tablespoon plus 1 teaspoon baking
   powder

1/2 teaspoon baking soda

1/2 teaspoon salt

1 tablespoon sugar

4 large eggs

2 cups whole milk

2 cups buttermilk

4 tablespoons (1/2 stick) unsalted butter,
   melted

Preheat the oven to 375°F. Grease a 2-quart casserole dish. Mix all the ingredients together in a large bowl with a whisk and pour into the casserole dish. Bake for 55 to 60 minutes, until browned and puffy. The center will be custardlike.

SAUSAGE CORNBREAD

SERVES 8

You can make a spicy version of this recipe by using a hot version of pork sausage.

1 pound ground pork sausage

2 large eggs

1 1/2 cups self-rising cornmeal

1 (15 1/4-ounce) can cream-style corn

3/4 cup whole milk

1/4 cup vegetable oil

1 large sweet onion, chopped

2 cups grated Cheddar cheese

Preheat the oven to 425°F. Grease a 10-inch cast-iron skillet and set aside. In another skillet, brown the sausage over medium-high heat; drain well and set aside. In a medium bowl, combine the eggs, cornmeal, corn, milk, and oil. Pour half of the cornmeal mixture into the cast-iron skillet. Layer the chopped onion over the cornmeal mixture; add the sausage and the cheese. Pour the remaining cornmeal mixture over the cheese (do not stir). Bake for 30 to 40 minutes, until puffed and browned.

MAMA'S SPOON ROLLS

MAKES 18 ROLLS

2 cups warm (100° to 110°F) water

1 package active dry yeast

1/4 cup sugar

3/4 cup vegetable oil

1 large egg, lightly beaten

4 cups self-rising flour

Preheat the oven to 425°F. Grease a 12-cup muffin tin. In a large bowl, combine the yeast and warm water. Using a sturdy wooden spoon, add the remaining ingredients and mix well. Fill the cups of the muffin tin half-full with batter. Bake for 20 minutes, or until the tops are lightly browned.

SWEET POTATO BISCUITS

MAKES ABOUT A DOZEN BISCUITS

Southerners love to cook sweet potatoes many different ways. The potato lends a texture and sweetness to the biscuit you'll love.

3 cups all-purpose flour

2/3 cup sugar

2 tablespoons baking powder

1/4 teaspoon baking soda

1 1/2 teaspoons salt

8 tablespoons (1 stick) unsalted butter

2 cups mashed sweet potatoes, baked

2 tablespoons buttermilk

Preheat the oven to 400°F. Grease a baking sheet and set aside. Sift together the flour, sugar, baking powder, baking soda, and salt. Cut in the butter with your fingers or 2 forks until the mixture resembles coarse cornmeal. Add the sweet potatoes, stirring well to combine. Gradually add the buttermilk to form a soft dough. Turn out onto a lightly floured board. Pat the dough into a 1/2-inch-thick circle and cut out the dough with a 3-inch biscuit cutter. Place on the baking sheet. Bake for 18 to 20 minutes, until the bottoms are lightly browned.

A GRAND PIANO

The piano has been a fixture of Mary Mac's dining room for decades, and is now used mainly for parties and special group functions. For many years, though, it sat in the dining room and inspired some customers and musicians to serenade the crowd. When Frances Rowland of Stone Mountain passed away recently, her obituary noted that she was a classically trained musician who had originally played in silent movie theaters, at church, and even at Mary Mac's.

"In her 80s, she went to Mary Mac's for lunch. They had a piano there, and she asked if it would be okay for her to play while people were eating," her son said. She loved to entertain the guests while she was there, and they loved listening to her.

PECAN PIE MUFFINS

MAKES 6 MUFFINS

I tasted these muffins at a wedding reception and frantically asked around as to who had made them so I could get the recipe for Mary Mac's. They are the creation of Lillian "Tigger" Megonegal.

1 cup chopped pecans, mixed, with
   1 tablespoon melted butter
1/2 cup all-purpose flour
1 cup firmly packed brown sugar

2 large eggs, lightly beaten
8 tablespoons (1 stick) salted butter,
   melted

Preheat the oven to 300°F. Spread the buttered pecans on a baking sheet and toast in the oven for 4 to 6 minutes, until fragrant; remove from the oven and let cool slightly.

Increase the oven temperature to 350°F. Line a 6-cup muffin tin with paper liners and coat with cooking spray. Combine the toasted pecans, flour, and brown sugar in a bowl. Make a well in the center of the dry ingredients; add the eggs and the melted butter and mix just until the dry ingredients are moistened. Spoon the batter into the paper-lined muffin cups, filling three-quarters full. Bake for 20 to 25 minutes, until the tops are lightly browned. Remove from the pan immediately to a wire rack and let cool completely.

"I've worked here for thirty-seven years. My mother and all my children worked here, too. Mary Mac's has been part of my family, so to speak."

— FLO PATRICK

BAKED APPLE PANCAKE

SERVES 6 TO 8

3 large Granny Smith apples, peeled,
   cored, and thinly sliced

2 teaspoons ground cinnamon

1/2 cup granulated sugar

1/2 cup firmly packed light brown sugar

1 cup whole milk

4 large eggs

2 teaspoons pure vanilla extract

1 cup all-purpose flour

Pinch of salt

4 tablespoons (1/2 stick) unsalted butter

Preheat the oven to 425°F. Lightly oil a 10-inch cast-iron skillet. Combine the apple slices, the cinnamon, and the sugars in a medium bowl. Put the milk, eggs, and vanilla into a blender and process until well mixed. Add the flour and a pinch of salt and process until smooth.

Melt the butter in the prepared skillet over medium heat. Add the apple mixture and cook, stirring occasionally, until the sugars have melted and the apples are well coated and softening, about 5 minutes. Gently pour the batter over the apples and place the skillet in the oven. Bake until the pancake is puffed, the edges are golden, and the apples are tender, 20 to 30 minutes. Serve immediately.

BANANA BREAD

MAKES 1 LOAF

1/2 cup vegetable shortening

1 cup sugar

2 large eggs, lightly beaten

1 3/4 cups all-purpose flour

1 teaspoon baking soda

1 teaspoon pure vanilla extract

3 to 4 ripe bananas, mashed

Preheat the oven to 350°F. Grease an 8 by 4-inch loaf pan. In the work bowl of a stand mixer, combine the shortening, sugar, and eggs. With the paddle attachment, on medium speed, mix in the flour and baking soda, beating until blended. Add the vanilla and bananas and mix well. Pour into the loaf pan. Bake for 1 hour.

Let cool in the pan. Transfer to a wire rack and let cool completely.

SEAFOOD

❖

Plus celebrities, politicians,

businessmen, writers,

photographers, teachers,

and even a gorilla

❖

CLOCKWISE FROM TOP LEFT: TED DANSON AND FAMILY; JOE PATTEN, OF THE FOX THEATRE, WHO HAS DINED WITH US FOR FIFTY-SIX YEARS; TIM CONWAY AND HARVEY KORMAN; ACTRESS ESTHER ROLLE AND JOHN FERRELL; MISS MAY AND MARTHA WEST, WHO ALWAYS CAME AT THE SAME TIME EACH DAY—10:55 A.M.

OUR CUSTOMERS

EACH DAY Mary Mac's serves hundreds—sometimes thousands—of diners. In a city as large as Atlanta, it would be easy to assume that we didn't need to work to keep our regular customers; that with a large population, healthy tourism, and nearby downtown businesses, we could simply sit on our laurels and maintain a good business. Perhaps we could, but that is not what our mission is at Mary Mac's. We take it seriously when we claim to be Atlanta's dining room. Our customers are treated like family, and, like family, we want them to enjoy the experience enough to come back again and again.

Every successful restaurant has a loyal following. An owner hopes that his regular customers will keep coming back, not only because it's financially healthy to have a fan base, but because it's a benchmark of how well the restaurant is being run.

Without really knowing it, our loyal customers become an extension of my and the manager's eyes and ears. If I don't see a regular guest for a few weeks, then I think perhaps I'd better look at what we're doing and if the problem might be ours.

Although I kept the bigger part of Mary Mac's the same, some features were added to make the restaurant my own. I put up a white picket fence around the parking lot. My dad rooted the red-buds, gardenias, and crepe myrtles for planting along the fence. Some of

his flowers grace the cover of this book. White napkins replaced the brown fingertip towels. I planted peach trees near the back door. The dining rooms, once known only as One, Two, Three, and Four, were finally given names: the Atlanta Room, the Myrtle Room, the Ponce Room, and the Skyline Room. Today, we have six dining rooms. We added the Ferrell Room and the Board Room, and renamed the bar, Ferrell's Bar. I made this last change to get my father involved in the business—I knew he was capable of pouring a drink! The Atlanta Room has been updated with a wall-length mural of the Carter Center grounds, and the Atlanta skyline mural still graces the Skyline Room.

Extensive renovations were completed that first year, culminating in a new central foyer that pulled together the old storefronts that had been tacked on over the years of growth. The new foyer opened a straight view down the center of the restaurant. You could often find me in the foyer, seating guests and looking down to the Ponce Room, where Charlotte Smith, a longtime employee, would stand. I would hold up the number of fingers to tell her how many were in a party and, in return, would receive a signal from a light panel on the wall as to which dining room had space.

I also began to keep the restaurant open on the weekends. To encourage after-church diners, I originally announced that I would donate 10 percent of the check amount to patrons' churches if they brought their Sunday bulletins. I faithfully sent in money to dozens of churches twice a year. It was only a matter of time before congregations all over midtown Atlanta were hearing their ministers close sermons with the exhortation to "go eat lunch at Mary Mac's and don't forget your bulletin!" Sundays quickly became the busiest day of the week.

In addition to the renovations I made to the building, I converted the old take-out cafeteria space into my office. After working in the space for a while, I realized it would be better used as a small private dining room. Today, this space is utilized as an office to accommodate our growing banquets and catering business. It is not uncommon for Mary Mac's to book events for up to 1,000 guests off site as well as host groups as large as 250 in house.

Mary Mac's has meant many things to many people, but more importantly it's become one of the most memorable and venerated landmarks in Atlanta—a destination for Atlantans and visitors from around the world who are looking for an authentic taste of the South. Visitors enter its doors in anticipation of the famous fried chicken, fresh greens, fried green tomatoes, and other favorites. Longtime residents head straight there after church for honest food that makes the South feel like the

South again. For Southerners, traditional food is the stuff of comfort and memories. Mary Mac's is the only restaurant that can provide both in abundance.

The interesting thing about Mary Mac's customers is you can't categorize them. We serve people from all walks of life, the rich and poor, teachers, celebrities, politicians, young and old, black and white.

Coach Leonard Hamilton, Florida State University's men's basketball coach, is a favorite customer, booking Mary Mac's for his team whenever they're in town for games against Georgia Tech. He says, "I never go to Atlanta without stopping by Mary Mac's. All my friends know if we go out to eat, there's no question of where we'll go. Mary Mac's is my home away from home."

Most major political figures in the South have ordered plates of Southern food at Mary Mac's while attempting to solve the problems of the day. With the tea room's close proximity to the state capitol, Georgia legislators often run in hungry and stroll out satisfied and ready for their afternoon session.

"It's convenient to the capitol and has wonderful food," says former Georgia governor Carl Sanders. "It is frequented during the legislative session by many members of the House and Senate and other state officials."

Some of the politicians we have enjoyed serving include former governors Sanders and Barnes, Senator Max Cleland, former first lady Hillary Clinton, Governors Sonny Perdue and Zell Miller, Lester Maddox, Hosea Williams, Jesse Ventura, Congressman John Lewis, Commissioner Nellie Duke, state representative Kathy Ashe, and many more.

Former senator Max Cleland and his family have frequented Mary Mac's for many years. During his Senate campaign in 1996, Cleland got in some last-minute campaigning in Mary Mac's dining rooms. It may just have done the trick—Cleland won by about 28,000 votes and went on to give his victory address to reporters from Mary Mac's. He is a special friend.

On May 2, 1995, First Lady Hillary Clinton dropped in at Mary Mac's with her large entourage for a scheduled round-table discussion with working women and a "to go" order of fried chicken, sweet potatoes, and sweet tea. During the round-table, Mrs. Clinton happily sampled the pound cake while discussing women's and children's issues.

Former Georgia governor Lester Maddox, himself the owner of a famous restaurant, celebrated both his eightieth and eighty-fifth birthdays at Mary Mac's Tea Room. He often ate at Mary Mac's, and chose the restaurant to celebrate these special occasions. His official eightieth birthday party was held at the Governor's Mansion, but he partied quite a bit at the tea room the week before. He played his harmonica with great animation for a visiting church group and was heard saying, "Meeting people, pleasing people, serving people, giving 'em a laugh, isn't it fun?" His eighty-fifth birthday party in September 2000 consisted of twenty people, including many prominent Georgia politicians. He and his political buddies shared lunch and memories over the Southern food.

President Jimmy Carter ate at Mary Mac's Tea Room so often that he even had a dessert named after him. Margaret Lupo introduced the peanut custard when Carter was running for governor. Then it was called "Jimmy Carter

GENE LUCKEY AND NANCY SHAIDNAGLE ARE TWENTY-FIVE-YEAR CUSTOMERS AND FRIENDS WHO HELPED ME REOPEN MARY MAC'S. THEY CLAIM OURS IS "THE BEST DANG SOUTHERN FOOD YOU CAN GET IN THE CITY OF ATLANTA." THEIR FRIEND DIANE SIMONE, AN EXECUTIVE PRODUCER AT TURNER BROADCASTING, IS A TWENTY-YEAR CUSTOMER. SHE SAYS, "THIS IS DECADENT FOOD!"

Custard." The name was changed to the grander "Presidential Pudding" as Carter's campaign for the White House began in the mid-1970s. After he won, it became "President's Pudding," and after his term was over, it was simply called "Carter Custard." When President Carter visits these days, he's often known to graciously make a special point of talking with children who are dining with their parents at tables around the room.

Mary Mac's has become a destination for notable international visitors. Romanian president Emil Constantinescu dined at the suggestion of Georgia Court of Appeals judge Dorothy Beasley, during his visit to Atlanta in 1999.

In 1977, Princess Asiy and Prince Faisal of Saudi Arabia ate here and tipped the waitress $100. The shocked waitress promptly fainted and had to be dragged into the kitchen before we could revive her!

The restaurant has always been a lunch destination for businessmen, and we count among our customers some of Atlanta's best-known leaders: Ted Turner; Douglas Ivester, CEO of Coca-Cola, who commissioned the wonderful Coca-Cola mural to be painted on the west wall of Mary Mac's and provided many historic photos of Atlanta that hang on our walls; Dr. William Suttles, president emeritus of Georgia State University.

Celebrities are often spotted at Mary Mac's. We've fed many stars, including Ted Danson, Cher (she ordered take-out fried chicken), Richard Gere, the Dalai Lama, Britney Spears (she sent her limo to pick up her order), Jessica Tandy, who ate here while filming *Driving Miss Daisy*, Tim Conway, Harvey Korman, Lily Tomlin (who came in disguise), and the famed Mississippi Mass Choir (all 103 of them), who stopped in during one of their tours and sang gospel music on request for the rest of the lucky diners present.

Our walls tell the story of the decades of celebrities who've dined at Mary Mac's—James Brown, American Idol Paris Bennett, actor Richard Thomas, Leonard Nimoy, Johnny Mercer, and Tom Poston are a few you'll spot.

Then there are the dedicated customers who have been coming to Mary Mac's for decades. Occasionally we will sadly read an obituary for one of the older patrons that will often mention that he or she was a regular at Mary Mac's.

Margaret Lupo introduced the peanut custard when Carter was running for governor. Then it was called "Jimmy Carter Custard." The name was changed to the grander "Presidential Pudding" as Carter's campaign for the White House began in the mid-1970s. After he won, it became "President's Pudding," and after his term was over, it was simply called "Carter Custard."

A piano teacher who retired in 1981, Frances Rowland kept coming to lunch at Mary Mac's through her eighties because she enjoyed playing the piano for other diners.

Judson Moses, a field representative for Metro-Goldwyn-Mayer, dined with his father every night for a decade at Mary Mac's, until Mr. Moses Sr. died in 1992 at the age of 104. Judson passed away in 2004 at the age of 81.

Joe Patten, often called the Phantom of the Fox because he lives in a secret apartment within the theater, has been dining with us for fifty-six years. Although he has slowed somewhat now that he's in his eighties, he used to walk the three blocks from the Fox Theatre for both lunch and dinner.

Throughout this book, I have included tidbits about some of our most loyal customers, people who have stories to tell about how Mary Mac's has become a part of their lives. I'm proud to be a part of so many lives, and I look forward to meeting many new friends in the coming years at Mary Mac's.

COACH HAMILTON OF FLORIDA STATE UNIVERSITY'S MEN'S BASKETBALL TEAM ENJOYS CORNBREAD
MUFFINS AT A RECENT VISIT TO MARY MAC'S. HE IS A REGULAR CUSTOMER WHENEVER HE'S IN TOWN,
AND HAS BEEN KNOWN TO BRING THE TEAM IN TO EAT AFTER A GAME.

GRILLED SALMON WITH ROASTED VEGETABLES

SERVES 4

1 zucchini, thinly sliced
1 yellow squash, thinly sliced
1 green pepper, chopped
1 red pepper, chopped
1 large sweet onion, chopped
20 to 24 small red potatoes, scrubbed
and the skin left on, halved or quartered

1/4 cup olive oil
Salt and freshly ground pepper
4 (6- to 8-ounce) fresh salmon fillets
Freshly squeezed lemon juice (optional)

Preheat the oven to 425°F. Preheat the grill to 400°F.

Place all the vegetables in a 13 by 9-inch baking dish and toss with the olive oil. Season with salt and pepper. Place in the oven for 45 to 50 minutes, until the potatoes are golden brown and the vegetables are slightly browned on the edges.

Approximately 10 minutes before the vegetables are ready, place the salmon fillets on the grill and grill on one side for no more than 4 minutes; turn and grill on the other side for 3 minutes. Remove from the grill, sprinkle with salt and add freshly squeezed lemon juice to taste, if desired. Serve immediately with the roasted vegetables.

SHRIMP AND GRITS

SERVES 6 TO 8

Fresh shrimp and that Southern staple grits create a unique and hearty meal when combined. This can be enjoyed at breakfast, lunch, or dinner.

4 cups water

3 cups quick white grits

4 cups shredded sharp Cheddar cheese

4 tablespoons (1/2 stick) salted butter

2 tablespoons blackening seasoning

2 pounds large tail-on shrimp, peeled
  and deveined

2/3 cup canola oil

1/2 cup finely chopped green bell pepper

1/2 cup finely chopped red bell pepper

1/2 cup finely chopped sweet onion

Bring the water to a boil over medium-high heat in a medium saucepan. Whisk in the grits, reduce the heat to medium-low, and cover. Cook, stirring every 3 to 4 minutes, until the liquid is absorbed and the grits are thick and creamy, about 20 minutes. Stir in the Cheddar cheese and butter; cover and reduce the heat to low.

Place the blackening seasoning in a bowl; add the shrimp and toss to coat. Heat half of the oil in a large sauté pan over medium-high heat. Sauté the bell peppers and onion until softened, 4 to 5 minutes. Transfer the vegetables to a bowl and keep warm.

Add the remaining half of the oil. Sauté the shrimp in batches for about 8 minutes, turning once, until pink and firm. Serve the shrimp over the grits; top with the vegetables.

SHRIMP JAMBALAYA

SERVES 4

4 tablespoons (1/2 stick) salted butter

1 tablespoon minced yellow onion

2 tablespoons all-purpose flour

1 cup whole milk

1 1/2 cups rice, cooked

1 1/2 cups large shrimp, lightly boiled and
  peeled

1/2 teaspoon celery salt

1 teaspoon salt

1/2 teaspoon freshly ground black pepper

1 teaspoon Worcestershire sauce

2 tablespoons canned tomato sauce

Melt the butter in a large, heavy skillet over medium-high heat. Sauté the onion until softened, about 1 to 2 minutes. Stir in the flour. Whisk in the milk until the mixture is smooth and the sauce is thickened and bubbling. Add the rice and shrimp. Reduce the heat and simmer. Add the celery salt, salt, pepper, Worcestershire sauce, and the tomato sauce. Simmer for 4 to 5 minutes and stir until just heated through. Serve immediately.

NAKED LUNCH

Margaret Lupo's favorite story, which she once told as a guest on Nathalie Dupree's television show (probably to Nathalie's chagrin!), involved a naked man.

One day at lunchtime, a man walked into Mary Mac's, went straight into one of the dining rooms, and started stripping his clothes off. Lupo heard a commotion and by the time she reached the dining room, the man was lying naked on the floor and wouldn't talk.

Lupo calmly covered him with an apron and had him hustled out the door.

When she returned to the dining room, an elderly customer motioned her over to her table, and naturally, Lupo was certain she would complain about the unseemly scene.

Instead, the woman told her, "Margaret, if you ever do this again, please get a man who's . . . Well, let's just say that if the floor show had been an entrée, I would have complained about the meager portions."

SALMON CROQUETTES

SERVES 6 (2 PATTIES PER SERVING)

1 red bell pepper, chopped

1 cup chopped green onions

1 cup mayonnaise

1/4 cup freshly squeezed lemon juice

2 teaspoons Chef Paul Prudhomme's
   Seafood Magic seasoning

1/2 teaspoon ground cayenne pepper

1 teaspoon salt

1/2 teaspoon freshly ground black pepper

8 large eggs, lightly beaten

4 (14 3/4-ounce) cans pink salmon,
   drained, boned, and flaked

3 cups dry or fresh bread crumbs

1 1/2 cups canola oil

Salt and freshly ground black pepper

Combine the red pepper, green onions, mayonnaise, lemon juice, seafood seasoning, cayenne pepper, salt, and the pepper in a bowl. Add the eggs, stirring to blend. Add the salmon and 1 cup of the bread crumbs and mix until blended.

Roll the mixture into 12 equal-sized balls. Dip each ball into the remaining 2 cups bread crumbs and flatten into patties. Pour 3/4 cup of the oil into a large sauté pan over medium-high and sauté the patties in batches for 2 minutes on each side or until golden brown. Repeat the procedure with the remaining 3/4 cup of oil and patties. Add salt and black pepper to taste.

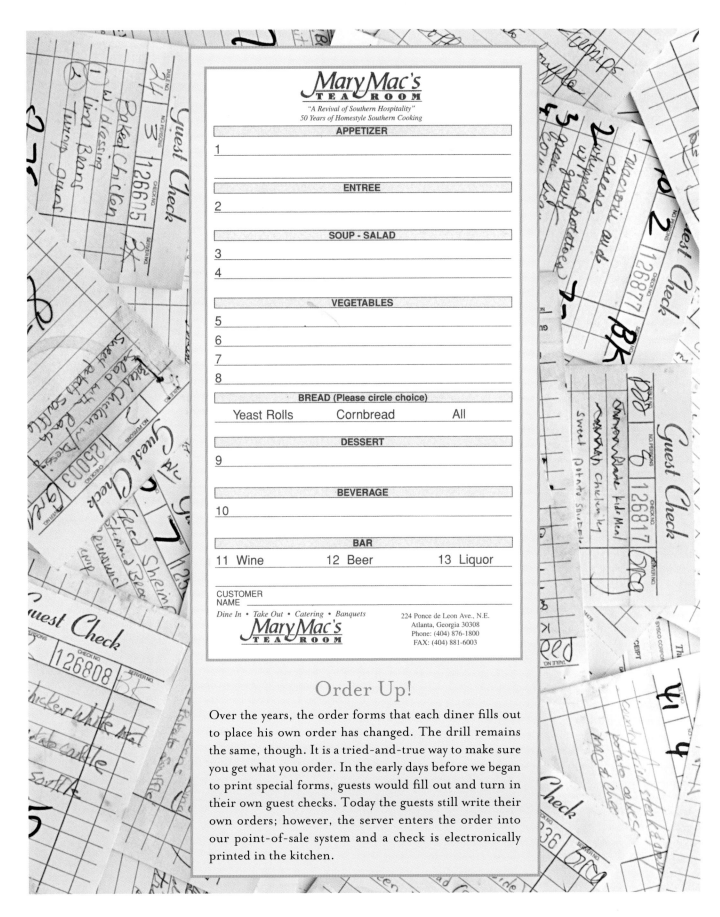

Mary Mac's
T E A • R O O M
"A Revival of Southern Hospitality"
50 Years of Homestyle Southern Cooking

APPETIZER

1 _____

ENTREE

2 _____

SOUP - SALAD

3 _____

4 _____

VEGETABLES

5 _____

6 _____

7 _____

8 _____

BREAD (Please circle choice)

Yeast Rolls   Cornbread   All

DESSERT

9 _____

BEVERAGE

10 _____

BAR

11 Wine   12 Beer   13 Liquor

CUSTOMER
NAME

Dine In • Take Out • Catering • Banquets

Mary Mac's
T E A • R O O M

224 Ponce de Leon Ave., N.E.
Atlanta, Georgia 30308
Phone: (404) 876-1800
FAX: (404) 881-6003

Order Up!

Over the years, the order forms that each diner fills out to place his own order has changed. The drill remains the same, though. It is a tried-and-true way to make sure you get what you order. In the early days before we began to print special forms, guests would fill out and turn in their own guest checks. Today the guests still write their own orders; however, the server enters the order into our point-of-sale system and a check is electronically printed in the kitchen.

RAINBOW TROUT

SERVES 4

Olive oil

4 fresh rainbow trout, heads removed, boned, and butterflied, with skin on

I teaspoon salt

I teaspoon freshly ground black pepper

Preheat the grill to medium-high (350° to 400°F). Lightly coat 4 sheets of aluminum foil with the oil. Place each trout on the foil; add the salt and pepper. Seal the edges of the foil. Place on the grill and grill, covered, for 10 to 12 minutes, until the fish flakes with a fork.

DEVILED CRAB

SERVES 4

Want to impress your guests hook, line, and sinker? Reserve the crab shells and serve the crab mixture in them. This is my mother, the late Mary Ferrell's recipe, and we offer this at Mary Mac's on special request.

I pound crabmeat, well-picked, and shredded, reserving 8 crab shells

I cup dry or fresh bread crumbs

2 large eggs, lightly beaten

1/2 cup minced celery

1/4 cup minced green bell pepper

1/4 cup minced red bell pepper

I tablespoon white vinegar

I tablespoon Worcestershire sauce

1/2 teaspoon hot sauce

2 tablespoons freshly squeezed lemon juice

8 tablespoons (I stick) salted butter, melted

I teaspoon dry mustard

1/2 teaspoon salt

1/2 teaspoon freshly ground black pepper

Preheat the oven to 375°F. Butter an 8 by 8-inch baking dish (if not using crab shells). Combine all the ingredients except the crab shells in a large bowl. Place the crab mixture in the baking dish, or in the 8 reserved crab shells. Bake for 10 to 12 minutes, until the crab mixture begins to brown. Serve immediately.

SALMON WITH MUSTARD AND SOY SAUCE

SERVES 4

The secret to this recipe is to marinate the salmon in the refrigerator before grilling.

1/3 cup olive oil

2 tablespoons Dijon mustard

2 tablespoons soy sauce

2 cloves garlic, minced

4 (6- to 8-ounce) salmon fillets

Salt

Freshly squeezed lemon juice

Combine the olive oil, mustard, soy sauce, and garlic in a small bowl. Place the salmon in a plastic freezer bag and pour the mustard-soy mixture over the salmon fillets, turning the freezer bag to coat. Marinate the salmon for 1 to 2 hours in a refrigerator. Remove the salmon from the bag and place onto a 400°F grill. Grill on one side for no more than 4 minutes, turn, and grill on the other side for 3 minutes. Remove from the grill and serve immediately. Sprinkle with salt and freshly squeezed lemon juice to taste, if desired.

GORILLAS IN OUR MIDST

Willie B., the gorilla who was for many decades the Atlanta Zoo's most famous resident—spawning a series of billboards with the question "Willie or Won't He?" when the zoo imported female gorillas so that he would produce an offspring—would seem to be an unlikely Mary Mac's fan.

After a visit to the restaurant, his trainer brought Willie B. some leftover cornbread one day. Willie took a great liking to the delicacy—in fact, he loved it so much that the trainer would often order loaves of cornbread by the dozens for the beloved gorilla.

"My job is to ensure that we continue to deliver on our promise of great food, served in a clean environment, with a large dose of Southern hospitality."

—MICHAEL FUHRMAN, General Manager

FRIED GULF SHRIMP AND OYSTERS

SERVES 6 TO 8

Vegetable oil

4 cups all-purpose flour

2 cups cornmeal

1 tablespoon salt

1 teaspoon white pepper

4 cups buttermilk

2 cups water

2 pounds freshly shucked oysters, drained

1 1/2 pounds large tail-on shrimp, peeled and deveined

Heat 1 inch oil in a heavy skillet over medium-high heat. Line a 15 by 10-inch rimmed baking pan with paper towels. Combine the flour, cornmeal, salt, and white pepper in a large shallow bowl. In a separate bowl, combine the buttermilk and water. Dip the oysters and shrimp into the buttermilk mixture. Dredge in the flour mixture, gently shaking off the excess flour. Place in a single layer on the pan.

Fry the oysters and shrimp in the hot oil for about 3 minutes, or until golden brown and the oysters and shrimp begin to float. Drain on paper towels; serve immediately.

CRAWFISH GUMBO

SERVES 6

4 tablespoons (1/2 stick) cup salted butter

1/3 cup all-purpose flour

1 cup chopped yellow onions

1 cup chopped celery

1 jalapeño pepper, seeded and sliced

2 cups water

3 cups crawfish tails

1 teaspoon salt

1 teaspoon freshly ground black pepper

1 (14 1/2-ounce) can crushed tomatoes, undrained

1 1/2 cups sliced okra

1 red bell pepper, chopped

1/4 cup chopped fresh parsley

2 teaspoons gumbo filé powder

3 cups hot cooked rice (optional)

Melt the butter in a large, heavy stockpot over medium-low heat. Add the flour and stir until the mixture turns dark brown, 10 to 15 minutes. Increase the heat to medium. Add the onions, celery, and jalapeño and cook, stirring, until crisp-tender, 2 to 3 minutes. Add the water, crawfish tails, tomatoes, salt, and pepper. Simmer for 15 minutes. Add the okra, bell pepper, and parsley. Simmer until the vegetables are crisp-tender, about 10 minutes. Stir in the filé powder. Ladle the gumbo into soup bowls and top with the rice.

PICKLES & CANNING

❦

Meet the

helping hands—

our staff and

servers

MISS G, GREETS CUSTOMERS WITH OPEN ARMS AND A BIG SMILE; SPECIAL SERVER MARION MIMS, LOWER RIGHT, ONCE ASKED RICHARD GERE TO MARRY HER; LOWER LEFT, SOME OF OUR DAY STAFF POSE IN FRONT OF THE COKE MURAL ON MARY MAC'S EXTERIOR WEST WALL.

OUR STAFF

I WAS FORTUNATE to inherit some very good staff from Margaret Lupo, even though the restaurant had been closed down for months before I bought and reopened it in 1994. Some of the staff returned upon hearing that their former employer would be helping me with the transition and that I was going to remain true to Mary Mac's tradition of home-style cooking in a friendly, comfortable atmosphere. In short, they hoped that the good jobs they had so loved would again be a possibility, and I was happy to have hands on board who knew how the restaurant worked.

We have a few people still serving and cooking at Mary Mac's who have been employed here longer than thirty-five years. They are valuable assets to my business, and they know that—at least, I do my best to make sure they know it. In each chapter of this book, we have included a portrait of some of our most important employees, the people who make things run smoothly and know how to handle our day-to-day operations.

Let me introduce you to some of the people you will meet when you visit Mary Mac's:

When you enter the front door, you'll most likely be greeted with open arms by "Miss G," Geraldine McTure, who started as a cashier and now serves as our hostess. Her face is the first you see when you come in the door, and she treats people with the graciousness for which Southerners are known. Miss G used to be a preschool teacher, so she works well under pressure, and she always, always, has a smile on her face. While you're having a friendly chat with her about your day, your health, or your business, you may not notice how quickly she is moving to find a table for you. She tries to get people seated as soon as possible so there's not a wait, and she's perfectly happy to bus tables if the situation calls for it. A guest recently brought Miss G an apple-crunch cake as a gift, because she was so enthusiastic about how well she and her friends had been treated at a previous visit to Mary Mac's. Miss G works our busy lunch shift and greets around 500 people each day.

When you're shown to a table, you may have the good luck to be waited on by one of our famous servers. Each of them has loyal customers who never fail to ask for them by name and might sometimes leave if their server's not available.

Born in Crawfordville, Georgia, Martha Evans has worked at Mary Mac's for thirty-seven years, since September 3, 1973. Martha has always been a server during that time, although she does admit to having done a bit of kitchen prep early in her career. You will recognize her by the big earrings she wears daily—her collection was once the subject of an *Atlanta Magazine* article, "The Waitress with the Big Earrings." Martha has 450 pairs of earrings, and she prides herself on never wearing the same pair twice in a year.

Martha is a special waitress whose customers never fail to ask to be seated at one of her tables. She has two or three regular customers who have come to "sit with her" for almost twenty years. I think they enjoy her sunny disposition and her dependable greeting, "Whatcha gonna have, honey?"

Evelyn Stewart went to school with Martha Evans back in Crawfordville, Georgia, and has worked at Mary Mac's since November 21, 1975. She is one of our special waitresses now, but she has also bused tables, and served as cocktail waitress and then bartender before becoming a full-time server. She has been here so long that several of her old customers have passed on or retired; however, each day at 12:20 p.m. she serves the table of Georgia Tech professors. This group has been coming in for decades and they always sit at the same table in the Skyline Room—Evelyn's table.

Evelyn also proudly remembers waiting on President Carter and his family, as well as former Senator Max Cleland's mother who was a daily customer until she passed away.

Another server who has worked his way around the restaurant as host, bartender, and now server is James Green from Savannah, Georgia. He has only been with us for seven years, but has earned a special reputation for entertaining the celebrities who sometimes drop in for home cooking. He remembers serving Jane Fonda, Beyoncé's husband, Jay-Z, and Whitney Houston, who he reports likes to eat the all-veggie plate. James is a talented piano player who likes to perform Broadway show tunes and fellow Savannahian Johnny Mercer's songs. He plays our grand piano for special parties and functions, and says that one of his favorite groups is the Saint Patrick's Day Parade committee, who comes to meet and eat at Mary Mac's in the months before the parade.

Jo Carter, our "goodwill ambassador," is a native of West Virginia who came to Atlanta in 1962 and has worked at Mary Mac's since 1993. She has been a waitress, hostess, and manager. Jo retired in 2004 and moved back to West Virginia, but I needed her and thought she might be homesick for Mary Mac's, so I drove to West Virginia and asked her if she was "ready to come home." She decided she wanted to come back, but she asked if she could have a "special" job, not hostessing or serving as she'd done in the past. I came up with the idea of making Jo our "goodwill ambassador." Her job is to see that all our guests leave happy so they will be sure to return.

Jo took the task to heart and is known around town now as the "back rub lady" because of all the back massages she hands out during the course of the day. Making people happy is what she lives for, and we recently printed a T-shirt in her honor that said, "I got my belly filled and my back rubbed at Mary Mac's." Jo has become the face of Mary Mac's to many people who now call her "Miss Mary Mac."

Flo Patrick has waited on tables for thirty-seven years at Mary Mac's. Her mother worked at the tea room as a hostess and cashier, and in turn encouraged her daughter to work there. Flo's children have also worked at Mary Mac's, making it their own family tradition. When Flo lost her husband in 1992, she left the restaurant for a time. Her longtime customer Joe Patten told me at a party that I needed to get her back. He said, "Tell Flo I said that if she'll come back, I'll come eat with her." I called her, and, to my amazement and satisfaction, she agreed to return to Mary Mac's.

Flo has waited on her share of celebrities, including John Kerry's wife, Teresa Heinz, and Hillary Clinton, as well as local television personality, John Pruitt.

I hired Marion Mims as a server fifteen years ago. I knew her from a restaurant she worked at that was closing, and I chased her down to work for us. She likes to call the men "baby" and has been told, "I like that—my wife ain't called me baby in so long!" Marion is famous for asking Richard Gere to marry her while he was dining here. He said he'd get back to her on that, but I'm glad he hasn't.

Michael Fuhrman is our efficient and friendly general manager—you will probably never see him without a smile on his face.

"In addition to waiting tables, I'm the house piano player for special functions. I especially like to play Broadway show tunes and Johnny Mercer songs. I'm from Savannah and so is Johnny."
—JAMES GREEN

Bless him, I know that managing a restaurant this big, with this many employees, is not an easy job, but if anyone makes it look easy, that would be Michael.

Michael has been at Mary Mac's for less than two years. His duties include ensuring that we deliver on our promise of great food, served in a clean environment, with a large dose of Southern hospitality. He is responsible for keeping the traditions of the restaurant, and maintaining our reputation as Atlanta's dining room.

In the next chapter, you will meet the people in the kitchen—the talented cooks who prepare the vast quantities of food served daily.

APPLE BUTTER

MAKES ABOUT 4 HALF-PINT JARS

1 cup apple juice

3 pounds good cooking apples, peeled,
  cored, and cut into 8 wedges

3 cups sugar

2 teaspoons ground cinnamon

1 teaspoon ground nutmeg

1/2 teaspoon ground allspice

1/2 teaspoon ground cloves

2 tablespoons freshly squeezed lemon
  juice

Pinch of salt

In a blender, process 1/3 cup of the apple juice and 4 pieces of apple; process for 5 seconds. Repeat the procedure twice. Pour the mixture into a saucepan; add the sugar, spices, and lemon juice. Cook over low heat for about 45 minutes, or until thickened, stirring occasionally. Pour the hot mixture into clean, hot, sterilized glass half-pint jars, leaving 1/4-inch headspace. Wipe the jar rims. Top with the lids and rings and process for 10 minutes in a boiling-water canner. The apple butter can be eaten immediately.

BREAD AND BUTTER PICKLES

MAKES ABOUT 7 PINTS

4 pounds pickling cucumbers

4 medium yellow or sweet onions, halved
  and sliced 1/4 inch thick

1/2 cup plus 2 tablespoons salt

4 cups white vinegar

4 cups sugar

1 tablespoon white mustard seed

1 tablespoon ground turmeric

1 tablespoon celery seed

1/8 teaspoon ground cayenne pepper

Thinly slice the cucumbers. Place in a large Dutch oven. Add the onions and the 2 tablespoons salt and toss to combine. Let stand for 3 hours.

Drain the cucumber mixture, rinse, and drain again. Combine the vinegar, sugar, spices, and the 1/2 cup salt in a large, heavy saucepan; bring to a boil over medium-high heat. Add the cucumber mixture and return to a boil. Pack the vegetables and pour the hot liquid into clean, hot, sterilized glass pint jars, leaving 1/4-inch headspace. Wipe the jar rims. Top with the lids and rings and process for 10 minutes in a boiling-water canner. Let the cans sit for one week before using. Pickles will keep for up to a year.

PICKLED OKRA

MAKES ABOUT 5 PINTS

2 pounds fresh, tender okra, stemmed

5 small hot red or green peppers

5 cloves garlic, peeled

4 cups white vinegar

1/2 cup water

6 tablespoons salt

1 tablespoon celery seed

1 tablespoon mustard seed

Pack the okra pods into five clean, hot, sterilized glass pint jars. Put 1 of the hot peppers and 1 clove garlic in each jar. Combine the vinegar, water, salt, celery seed, and mustard seed in a saucepan; bring to a boil over medium-high heat and pour the hot liquid over the okra, leaving 1/4-inch headspace. Wipe the jar rims. Top with the lids and rings and process for 10 minutes in a boiling-water canner. Let stand for 8 weeks before using. This will keep for up to 12 months.

GREEN TOMATO PICKLES

MAKES ABOUT 15 PINTS

My aunt Bridget Chandler gave me this recipe after I almost drove her deaf asking for it—it's that good. The oil of cloves and oil of cinnamon are available from LorAnn Natural Flavoring Oils on Amazon.com, or you may order them from your local pharmacy.

7 pounds green tomatoes (no pink
   showing), sliced
1 1/2 cups pickling lime
5 pounds sugar

6 cups cider vinegar
2 or 3 drops oil of cloves
2 or 3 drops oil of cinnamon

Combine the green tomatoes and pickling lime in 2 gallons of cold water in a nonreactive container and let stand for 24 hours. Drain and place the tomatoes in a large nonreactive bowl.

In a large nonreactive pot, combine the sugar and vinegar and bring to a boil over medium-high heat. Turn the heat off and add the tomatoes to the liquid. Let stand overnight. The next morning, bring the mixture to a boil, cover, and cook for 1 hour over medium-high heat. Remove from the heat after 1 hour and stir in the oils, making sure to mix well.

Pack the tomatoes and pour the hot liquid into clean, hot, sterilized glass pint jars, leaving 1/2-inch headspace. Wipe the jar rims. Top with the lids and rings. Let stand for 14 days before using. Store the canned tomatoes in the pantry for up to 1 year.

Favorite Diners

Lee Fields and Clay Jones

"We moved to Atlanta from a small town in southern Georgia, so eating at Mary Mac's feels like a visit home. A few years ago, we lived in an apartment just behind the restaurant, and thought of this as our own dining room."

Lee worked for Mary Mac's for a while, and she attended Lester Maddox's birthday party at Mary Mac's. It was a celebration for the history books!

I hope their new son, Duncan, will be a regular Mary Mac's customer one of these days, too.

MARY MAC'S HOMEGROWN PEPPER SAUCE

On a trip to Mary Mac's a few years back, my father, John Ferrell Sr., did not like the pepper sauce on the table and told me frankly, "I can do better pepper sauce than that. You don't need to buy it anymore."

home and use for their own greens. This didn't much surprise my father. As he says, "Up here in Georgia, all these people like pepper sauce, and it seems like the hotter it is, the better they like it."

We decided to create a label for the sauce in 2002, and I transferred some of my father's pepper plants to my farm in North Carolina, to take over the production when he could no longer comfortably handle the physical work of producing so much of the pepper sauce himself.

I love growing the tasty little peppers and harvesting them for our sauce. The only hard part of the process is digging the plants out of the ground before the first freeze, so that we don't lose our crop. Sometimes the North Carolina winters sneak up on you, and I'll be out digging plants in the dark, to save them.

This was not an idle claim. John Sr.'s neighbors in rural Wakulla County, Florida, already knew him as the "pepper man." My father had over 100 tabasco pepper plants growing in his home garden.

I thought it was a great idea and jumped at my father's offer. So for years John Sr. typically made over 200 small jars of pepper sauce for the tea room annually. He also provided Mary Mac's with refill jugs of hot sauce, made with his home-grown tabasco peppers.

One year he made more than 300 bottles of pepper sauce and learned, to his delight, that customers were buying the bottles to take

Currently, we produce the sauce in the kitchen of Mary Mac's, bottling and labeling it ourselves. Although we've had offers to market the label nationally, I prefer to keep it a Mary Mac's exclusive. Customers who want to take some pepper sauce home with them can always purchase it at the restaurant.

PICKLES & CANNING

PEPPER SAUCE

MAKES 2 (10-OUNCE) CRUETS

My father always had a pepper garden when I was growing up and this was a permanent fixture on our table. I've made his pepper sauce a fixture on Mary Mac's tables, too.

2 cups (150 to 200 count) green
   Tabasco peppers (do not use
   jalapeños), stemmed

1 cup white vinegar
1/8 teaspoon salt

Rinse the peppers and set aside. (Wash your hands thoroughly after handling the peppers; do not touch your eyes.) Thoroughly wash 2 cruets or small bottles with stoppers. Rinse with very hot water, pack with the peppers, and set in a pan of hot water (to keep the glass from breaking). Pour the vinegar into a saucepan. Bring vinegar to a boil and pour the hot liquid over the peppers. (Use as much boiling vinegar as needed to fill the cruets.) Add 1/8 teaspoon salt in the top of each cruet. Place the stoppers on the bottles and let stand for 3 days before using. These will keep for up to 2 years.

PEPPER JELLY

MAKES ABOUT 4 HALF-PINT JARS

6 green bell peppers, chopped
1/4 pound hot green banana peppers
1 1/2 cups cider vinegar

6 1/2 cups sugar
1 (6-ounce) bottle liquid pectin

In a blender, process the bell peppers and hot peppers until smooth. In a saucepan, combine the vinegar and sugar and bring to a rolling boil over medium-high heat; boil for 2 minutes. Add the puréed peppers and liquid pectin and boil for 1 minute. Skim off the foam. Pour the hot mixture into clean, hot, sterilized glass half-pint jars, leaving 1/4-inch headspace. Wipe the jar rims. Top with the lids and rings and process for 10 minutes in a boiling-water canner.

– 118 –

SIDES

❧ ◆ ❧

Behind the scenes:

the hands that

stir the pots

❧ ◆ ❧

TOP LEFT, SHIRLEY MITCHELL (CENTER) WORKS ON THE LINE IN 1995; HIRED OUT OF RETIREMENT IN 1994, MINNIE GOODE, TOP RIGHT, SNAPS BEANS AND DOES ALL THE SALAD PREP WORK; ABOVE, CHEF DEREK CHECKS THE LINE ITEMS JUST BEFORE THE LUNCH CROWD ARRIVES.

IN THE KITCHEN

NATHALIE DUPREE, prominent cookbook author and television host, fondly recalls eating at Mary Mac's. "Margaret's cooking was true Southern cooking. Good biscuits, good cornbread, good okra. If she didn't have fresh, she didn't do it," Dupree says.

She took many well-known and famous food writers to Mary Mac's. "When people came to town and wanted real Southern food, I took them to Mary Mac's. They loved it," she remembers. Nathalie later asked Margaret to do a guest spot on her cooking show to showcase a few of Margaret's favorite recipes and cooking techniques.

Guests at Mary Mac's may feel like the food has been prepared just for them, but the truth of running such a large kitchen and feeding thousands each week calls for lots of help and a large grocery list. In addition to the tens of thousands of bunches of collard greens and green beans cooked, we use at least 90,000 pounds of flour and 75,000 pounds of sugar annually. All that is washed down with more than 10,000 gallons of sweet iced tea.

At any given moment, we have as many as twenty people cooking and working the kitchen. We have specialty cooks for cakes and pies, chicken and dumplings and fried chicken, and many other popular dishes. Most of the cooks are African American, and that's not unusual for Southern food or Southern kitchens. Many of the white women in the South learned to cook from the black help that were employed by families for generations. This meant that many of the same food traditions were passed down through both the black and white communities. Food is a shared experience in Atlanta, and the racial makeup of the dining guests at Mary Mac's has always reflected an appreciation of the same types of dishes.

For the first time since the restaurant opened, I have hired an executive chef, Derek Banks, to coordinate all the food preparation. Although I was hesitant to create this position after almost sixty years of operation, it may have been the best decision I've ever made!

Derek had more than twenty years experience as an executive chef and more than twenty-four years in the food industry when we hired him. He was comfortable feeding large crowds, and had cooked for 20,000 people at Bill Clinton's presidential election party in Little Rock, as well as feeding 30,000 at a Delta dinner at the World Congress Center. Derek has embraced the history and traditions of Mary Mac's and says of his responsibilities, "The spirit of Mary Mac's is inside me."

Derek has the chance to flex his creative chops in the kitchen with daily specials and Sunday brunch, and has created some new dishes that have been added to the menu. He tinkered with recipes that he felt could be better, such as the salmon croquettes. His new recipe has made that menu item one of the most popular. Other new dishes include fried perch, spiced pork chops, three-cheese meatloaf, and curried chicken.

Chef Derek oversees the kitchen, and manages all the people who work there, including the stewards, prep cooks, line guys, and supply person. All these people make sure that the forty-six items on our steam table are available at all times. He has won the respect of all the help in the kitchen with his professionalism and respect for the traditions at Mary Mac's.

On Thanksgiving Day, 2009, we served our first Thanksgiving dinner and fed 1,000 people. Because we had never been open on this holiday before, Derek gave each employee

Derek oversees the kitchen, and manages all the people who work there, including the stewards, prep cooks, line guys, and the supply person. All these people make sure that the forty-six items on our steam table are available at all times.

who had been with the restaurant more than fifteen years the option not to work that day. It was an example of the fairness that has won him a following with the cooks in the kitchen.

We are blessed with cooks who have been with Mary Mac's for a long spell; who have ensured that the food is dependably good on a daily basis. After all, what good is comfort food if it doesn't taste like your memory of it?

One of our important "quality controls" in the kitchen is Flora Hunter, who has been with us for thirty-five years, cooking her soufflés, meatloaf, chicken and dumplings, and bread pudding. Originally, she worked for Margaret Lupo, back when there were only two dining rooms. She is sixty-nine years young, and is one of the most dependable people we have. Derek Banks says, "Flora is the best employee I've ever had. She would come to work no matter the weather—I think she would come in a snowstorm!"

If you ask Flora what her best talent in the kitchen is, she'll say, "I can crack eggs faster than anyone." She's right, and you have to be fast to cook all that she does each week.

Another important cook in the kitchen is Shirley Ann Mitchell, who has also been with us for thirty-five years. She has worked all aspects of the kitchen—as a cook, baker, and line person. She has done it all! Her favorite thing is baking, and she will gladly tell you she is the best baker we have. Shirley is responsible

Mary Mac's Tea Room.
Luncheon

Thursday, April 19, 1956

Price below does not include Georgia State Sales Tax

No. 2 — $1.05

Tomato or Grapefruit Juice
ROAST SIRLOIN of WESTERN BEEF, Brown Gravy
BAKED CHICKEN and DRESSING, Cranberry Sauce
(All White Meat .40 extra)
HOME BAKED SUGAR CURED HAM
Choice of Two Vegetables, Coffee, Tea or Buttermilk
Choice of Dessert

No. 3 — 90c

CHICKEN PAN PIE
COUNTRY FRIED STEAK with GRAVY
Choice of Two Vegetables, Coffee, Tea or Buttermilk
Choice of Dessert

No. 4 — 75c

SPANISH MEAT SAUCE on SPAGHETTI, Parmesan Cheese
CREAMED CHIPPED BEEF on TOAST
Choice of Two Vegetables, Coffee, Tea or Buttermilk
Choice of Dessert

No. 5 — Vegetable Plate — 65c

CHOICE of THREE VEGETABLES
Dessert and Drink, Coffee, Tea or Buttermilk

Salads — 40c

Chopped Raw Vegetable, Roquefort Cheese Dressing
or 1000 Island Dressing

Vegetables — (Choice of Two)

Fresh String Beans   Sweet Potato Souffle, Marshmallow Topping
Fresh Mustard Greens   Au Gratin Potatoes
Succotash (Corn and Green Lima Beans)   Stewed Tomatoes
Chilled Sliced Cucumbers in Vinegar
Homemade Potato Salad   Pickled Beets   Rice and Gravy
Creamy Cottage Cheese   Chicken Dressing, Gravy
Macaroni and Cheese   Cole Slaw   Apple Sauce
Chopped Raw Vegetable Salad, French or 1000 Island Dressing,
Roquefort Cheese Dressing (.10 extra)

Desserts — 20c

Apple Cobbler   Baked Grapenut Pudding
Black Cherry Ice Cream   Fresh Strawberry Ice Cream
Plain Jello or Jello with Custard Topping
Boiled Custard
Chocolate, Vanilla or Almond Crunch Ice Cream
Margarine Served Here
Sweet Milk .10 extra

NO SUBSTITUTIONS WITHOUT EXTRA CHARGE

Mary Mac's

224 Ponce de Leon Avenue   Monday - Friday
Atlanta, Georgia 30308   Lunch: 11:00 am - 3:00 pm
Phone: 876-1800   Dinner: 5:00 pm - 9:00 pm
Fax: 881-6003   Closed Saturday & Sunday

Friday

Price Includes Sales Tax

LUNCHEON

FRESH VEGETABLE LUNCHEON 5.00
Choice of four side dishes
MARY MAC'S SOUTHERN LUNCHEONS
Entree with One Side Dish 6.00
Entree with Two Side Dishes 6.50
Entree with Three Side Dishes 7.00
Extra Side Dish (with Full Meal) 50
Soup and Salad 4.00
JUNIOR PLATE (Half Portions) 3.00
(For customers under 12 or over 90)
All These Meals Include Hot Breads and Choice of Coffee, Tea, or Punch

ENTREES

BAKED CHICKEN WITH CORNBREAD DRESSING AND GRAVY
FRIED CHICKEN, THREE LEGS OR ONE BREAST
(Child's Fried Chicken Plate, One Leg)
COUNTRY FRIED STEAK WITH GRAVY
BAR B Q PORK WITH BRUNSWICK STEW
BAKED OR FRIED FISH
CHEESE SOUFFLÉ WITH BACON STRIPS

SIDE DISHES

Cup of Fresh Homemade Vegetable Soup
Cup of Pot Likker with Cornbread

Creamed Corn	Whipped Potatoes
Steamed Broccoli	Green Lima Beans
Fresh String Beans	Macaroni and Cheese
Fresh Turnip Greens	Cornbread Dressing with Gravy
Rice with Gravy	Sweet Potato Souffle
Homemade Cole Slaw	Pickled Beets
Fresh Green Salad (1000, Bleu, Italian, French)	Potato Cakes
Apple Sauce	Cottage Cheese

DESSERTS

Boiled Custard	Carter Custard
Fruited Jello Salad	Plain Jello
Georgia Peach Cobbler	Homemade Poundcake with Strawberries and Cream

ICE CREAM

Vanilla	Chocolate
Almond Toffee	Tangerine Sherbert

"Table Wine of the South" (Sweet Tea) — $1.00

Small Sweet Milk	.50 extra	Small Buttermilk	.50 extra
Large Sweet Milk	1.00 extra	Large Buttermilk	1.00 extra
Coca-Cola or Diet Coke	1.00	Coffee, Tea, Punch	1.00

SINGLE CHOICES FROM ABOVE MENU —
Choice of Meat - 3.50   Choice of Vegetables — 1.00
Hot Breads — .25

Turnip Green Pot Likker — Bowl 1.50, Cup 1.00 (with Corn Muffins)
Homemade Vegetable Soup — Bowl 2.00, Cup 1.00 (with Saltines)
(with Corn Muffins — .15 each)

THE MENU FAR LEFT IS FROM THURSDAY, APRIL 19, 1956; THE OTHER IS A MENU FROM 1995. AS YOU CAN SEE, PRICES HAVE CHANGED THROUGH THE YEARS, BUT NOT MUCH OF ANYTHING ELSE HAS. THE SIZE OF THE MENU AND MANY OF THE ITEMS REMAIN THE SAME TODAY. OF COURSE, WE OFFER SPECIALS ALL THE TIME, AND WILL ADD SOMETHING TO THE MENU IF WE THINK IT'S A KEEPER. THE POPULAR TOMATO PIE WOULD BE A RECENT EXAMPLE OF A NEW ITEM ADDED TO THE MENU.

daily for all breads, pies and cakes, cinnamon rolls, and some other dishes, such as collards and greens.

The restaurant also runs a busy catering business. Fully one-quarter of our income comes from catering events and parties off-premises. Additionally, we have become a popular stop on motor coach tours that include CNN, the Georgia Aquarium, the Cyclorama, and the World of Coke, so we see quite a large number of tourists in the restaurant.

If it's hard to comprehend just how important it is to serve large quantities of comfort food daily for sixty-five years, and keep people coming back, just compare our menu from the 1950s with our menu today, half a century later. It's amazing that the items are so similar, and that the basic menu style has not changed over these many years. The prices, of course, have, but with inflation, a meal at Mary Mac's is still considered one of the best bargains in Atlanta. This consistency of menu attests to how well our cooks perform and how well they know good Southern food.

I think the biggest change in the kitchen has been that I am committed to providing better equipment to make everyone's job easier. Our kitchen staff has been quick to tell me how they appreciate this investment in their jobs, and equally gratifying is the fact that our business has grown because of this attention to detail.

"*My job for the last thirty-five years has been to make sure that the meatloaf, chicken and dumplings, and sweet potato soufflé taste the same as they always have.*
And I can crack eggs faster than anyone."

—FLORA HUNTER

WHITE LIMA BEANS AND HAM OVER RICE

SERVES 4

This classic Southern way to use a leftover ham bone is delicious served over white rice with cornbread and boiled turnips.

1 (16-ounce) package large lima beans, cooked according to package directions and drained

1 leftover ham bone with some meat remaining, or you may substitute 12 to 14 ounces fatback (salt pork)

2 1/2 teaspoons salt

1/2 teaspoon freshly ground black pepper

1/2 teaspoon sugar

5 tablespoons bacon drippings

6 cups water

Cooked rice

Place the cooked lima beans, ham bone, fatback, salt, pepper, sugar, and bacon drippings in a stockpot; add the water. Bring to a boil over medium-high heat and cook for 5 minutes. Reduce the heat to medium to medium-low and simmer for about 1 hour and 45 minutes, or until the beans are very tender. Taste the beans halfway through the cooking process and add more salt and pepper, if needed. Serve over rice.

Favorite Diners

Tommie Nichols

"Growing up, my parents brought me often to Mary Mac's. The yeast rolls were my favorite since as far back as I can remember. I met John Ferrell thirty-two years ago, before he bought the restaurant, and his owning it makes it seem like visits are still a family affair. For those of us who have lived in Atlanta all our lives, Mary Mac's is a generational experience."

TOMATO PIE

SERVES 10 TO 12

Mary Mac's added this dish to the menu in 2009 and it has quickly risen into the top five side dishes ordered. This is, by far, our most requested recipe.

2 tablespoons olive oil
2 medium sweet onions, thinly sliced
Salt and freshly ground black pepper
1 box Ritz crackers
2 (28-ounce) cans diced tomatoes, undrained

2 cups mayonnaise
1 1/2 cups grated extra sharp Cheddar cheese
1 cup grated Parmesan cheese
3 tablespoons chopped fresh basil

Preheat the oven to 350°F. Grease a 13 by 9-inch baking dish with olive oil or butter. Heat the 2 tablespoons olive oil in a large skillet over medium heat; add the onions and cook, stirring occasionally, until soft and translucent, 4 to 5 minutes. Add the salt and pepper to taste, remove from the heat, and set aside.

Crush 2 sleeves of Ritz crackers by hand or in a food processor. Reserve 1/2 cup of the cracker crumbs for the topping. Place half of the remaining cracker crumbs in the bottom of the baking dish and pour 1 can of the diced tomatoes, with juice, over the cracker crumbs. Layer half of the the sautéed onions on top of the tomatoes, and repeat the layering process using the rest of the tomatoes and onions. Sprinkle the remaining half of the cracker crumbs over the tomato mixture.

In a bowl, combine the mayonnaise, Cheddar cheese, Parmesan cheese, and basil. Spread the mixture over the layers and sprinkle the reserved 1/2 cup cracker crumbs on top. Bake for 30 to 40 minutes, until the top is golden brown.

FRIED GREEN TOMATOES

SERVES 6

These are not hard to make. Just use fresh-cut and locally grown green tomatoes, lightly bread them, and fry to a golden brown. How many other recipes are worthy of a movie?

2 cups vegetable oil

1 large egg

2 tablespoons whole milk

1 teaspoon salt

1/4 teaspoon freshly ground black pepper

1 cup all-purpose flour

1/4 cup cracker crumbs

3 firm medium green tomatoes, cut into
   1/4-inch slices

Heat the vegetable oil in a deep-fryer or in a heavy, deep skillet to 350°F. Line a plate with paper towels. In a small bowl, beat the egg; add the milk, 1/2 teaspoon of the salt, and the black pepper. In a separate bowl, combine the flour, cracker crumbs, and the remaining 1/2 teaspoon salt. Dip the tomato slices into the egg mixture, turning to coat. Dredge in the flour mixture until well coated. Place in the hot oil and fry until golden brown, turning once. Drain. Serve immediately.

BAKED EGGPLANT WITH CHEDDAR

SERVES 4 TO 6

1 medium eggplant, peeled and diced into 1-inch cubes

2 large eggs, lightly beaten

3/4 cup whole milk

4 tablespoons (1/2 stick) salted butter, melted

1/2 cup bread crumbs

1/2 cup diced yellow onion

Dash of hot sauce

3/4 cup grated sharp Cheddar cheese, plus 2 tablespoons

1 cup saltine crackers, crushed

Preheat the oven to 350°F. Butter a 2-quart casserole dish. Place the eggplant and water to cover in a small saucepan, and cook over medium-low heat for 15 minutes; drain.

In a large bowl, combine the eggplant, eggs, milk, melted butter, bread crumbs, onion, hot sauce, and cheese. Pour the eggplant mixture into the casserole dish. Sprinkle the cracker crumbs evenly over the mixture. Bake for 30 to 40 minutes, until bubbly and golden brown. Sprinkle 2 tablespoons of the grated cheese on top about 10 minutes before done.

BLACK-EYED PEAS

SERVES 4 TO 6

Black-eyed peas are considered good luck on New Year's Day, a tradition supposedly dating back to the Civil War, when Union troops would strip the countryside of all stored food and destroy whatever they couldn't carry away. Northerners didn't consider "field peas" or field corn suitable to eat, and left those humble foods in the field.

1 small smoked ham hock

5 ounces fatback (salt pork)

1 small yellow onion, diced

4 cups dried black-eyed peas

1/2 teaspoon white pepper

Bring a stockpot two-thirds full with water to a boil over medium-high heat. Add the ham hock, fatback, and onion and return to a rolling boil. Add the black-eyed peas and let cook, uncovered, for approximately 1 hour, or until the black-eyed peas are tender. Add salt and pepper if desired. Serve with a slotted spoon.

BROCCOLI CASSEROLE

SERVES 8

2 (10-ounce) packages frozen chopped
  broccoli
1 cup shredded Cheddar cheese
1 cup mayonnaise
2 large eggs, lightly beaten
1 1/2 tablespoons salted butter

1 1/2 tablespoons all-purpose flour
1 1/2 cups whole milk
1 tablespoon chopped sweet onion
1 sleeve Ritz crackers, crushed
2 tablespoons salted butter, cut into
  small pieces

Preheat the oven to 350°F. Butter a 3-quart casserole dish. In a large bowl, mix together the broccoli, cheese, mayonnaise, and eggs. In a large sauté pan over medium heat, melt 1 1/2 tablespoons of the butter; whisk in the flour. Let cook for 2 minutes, or until foamy. Slowly whisk in the milk until smooth. Return to a boil, stirring until thickened. Remove from the heat and let cool slightly before stirring into the broccoli mixture. Pour the broccoli mixture into the casserole dish and sprinkle with the crushed crackers. Dot the top with the 2 tablespoons butter. Bake for 30 minutes, or until bubbly and golden brown.

HOPPIN' JOHN

SERVES 4 TO 6

You must eat Hoppin' John on New Year's Day if you're a Southerner. It's black-eyed peas all "gussied up" for the holiday!

8 cups water
1 pound quick-cooking rice
1 recipe Black-Eyed Peas (page 129),
  warmed

In a large saucepan, bring the water to a boil over medium-high heat. Add the rice and cook for 5 to 10 minutes, until tender. Add the warm black-eyed peas to the rice. Serve immediately.

CHEESE AND VEGETABLE SOUFFLÉ

SERVES 8

This recipe is one I tasted on a trip to Savannah, Georgia. I offered it as a special at Mary Mac's and it quickly became so popular that we added it to the permanent menu.

1/4 cup olive oil

6 medium yellow squash, sliced

2 medium zucchini, sliced

2 medium sweet or yellow onions, chopped

1 cup chopped red bell pepper

1/2 cup chopped yellow bell pepper

1/2 cup chopped green bell pepper

1 cup fresh corn cut from the cob

1/4 teaspoon salt

5 large eggs

3 cups heavy cream

2 teaspoons hot sauce

5 cups shredded sharp Cheddar cheese

2 sleeves (8 ounces) Ritz crackers, crushed

3 tablespoons salted butter, melted

Preheat the oven to 350°F. Butter a 13 by 9-inch baking dish. Heat the olive oil in a large sauté pan over medium-high heat. Add the vegetables and salt, and cook, stirring frequently, until softened, about 10 minutes. In a large bowl, combine the eggs, heavy cream, and hot sauce, and mix well. Set aside. Layer the bottom of the baking dish with half of the vegetables, then top with a layer of Cheddar cheese; repeat with a second layer of vegetables and Cheddar cheese. Pour the cream mixture into the baking dish over the vegetable and cheese layers and top with the cracker crumbs. Drizzle the top with the melted butter and bake for 45 minutes, or until bubbly and golden brown.

COLLARD GREENS

SERVES 6 TO 8

2 1/2 pounds collard greens, washed, stalks and stems removed, and leaves cut into 2-inch strips

2 tablespoons salt

2 gallons water

1 smoked ham hock

6 ounces fatback (salt pork)

1/3 cup bacon drippings

Wash the cut collards in cold water. Drain and repeat with the 2 tablespoons salt added. Let soak for 10 minutes. The salt will eliminate any pest that may have decided to stay on the washed greens. Drain. Repeat and wash again if needed to make sure all the grit and dirt is removed. It is not uncommon to have to wash greens multiple times to ensure that all grit/sand is removed. Bring the 2 gallons water to a boil in a large stockpot; add the ham hock and fatback and let boil for 1 hour. Add the collards and bacon drippings to the broth. Return to a rolling boil; reduce the heat to a simmer and cook for 40 to 45 minutes. Add additional water if the water starts to absorb past one-third of the original broth level. Remove from the heat and serve with John Ferrell's Cornbread (see page 72). For an additional kick, add a dash or two of pepper sauce.

THE QUEEN OF GREENS

So popular are the greens and pot likker at Mary Mac's that during her ownership, Margaret Lupo was dubbed the "Queen of Greens." Each year, Mary Mac's cooks up 7,500 bunches of collard greens, and hundreds of bowls of pot likker are served weekly.

For out-of-town visitors not acquainted with the likes of pot likker, *Sky* magazine noted in their November 1999 issue, "The most divine Dixie delight is pot likker—a salubrious pine-green soup retrieved from the pot in which greens have long been simmered with a hunk of ham bone. . . . Its powerhouse vegetable savor is intoxicating." Such strong words would lead you to believe that the simple soup is not for the faint of heart, nor the unsuspecting visitor from the north.

Not so, or at least not according to Calvin Trillin, well-known New York author. When he visited the city some years ago, he asked where the best restaurants in Atlanta were, and was directed to some of our more posh eateries serving continental cuisine. Why, he later wondered, wasn't he directed to a place like Mary Mac's, where "you could get a good bowl of greens and cornbread?" Come on down anytime, Calvin!

POT LIKKER

SERVES 6 TO 8

First-time guests at Mary Mac's receive a complimentary cup of our pot likker, which is the juice from the greens that are prepared fresh daily. Crumble some cornbread in it for a delicious treat.

1 ounce fatback (salt pork), diced

2 cups chicken broth

2 cups water

1 cup cooked turnip greens and their juices

Salt

White pepper

Hot sauce or Pepper Sauce (see page 118)

In a heavy skillet over medium-high heat, fry the diced fatback until browned, reducing the heat, if necessary, to prevent overcooking. In a stockpot, combine the fatback and pan drippings, broth, water, and turnip greens and juice. Bring to a boil, reduce the heat to a simmer, and cook for 5 minutes, or until heated through. Add salt, white pepper, and hot sauce or Pepper Sauce to taste. Serve hot.

CORNBREAD DRESSING AND CHICKEN GRAVY

SERVES 6 TO 8

3 large eggs

2 cups chicken broth

I teaspoon salt

1/2 teaspoon white pepper

1/2 cup chopped yellow or sweet onion

1/2 cup chopped celery

4 tablespoons (1/2 stick) butter, melted

6 cornbread muffins (see page 72)

5 slices day-old white bread, cut into
   I-inch cubes

Chicken Gravy (recipe follows)

Preheat the oven to 350°F. Lightly grease a 2-quart baking dish. In a large bowl, whisk the eggs; stir in the chicken broth, salt, white pepper, onion, celery, and melted butter. Crumble the cornbread into the mixture and add the white bread cubes. Let the mixture stand for 30 minutes.

Spoon the dressing mixture into the baking dish and bake for 30 minutes, or until set and puffed. Serve with warm chicken gravy.

CHICKEN GRAVY

(Makes about 2 cups)

2 cups broth, reserved from Baked
   Chicken (page 34), or purchased

3 tablespoons all-purpose flour

I cup whole milk

I cup water

1/2 teaspoon salt

1/8 teaspoon white pepper

Freshly ground black pepper (optional)

I tablespoon salted butter (optional)

In a small saucepan, heat the 1/2 cup reserved giblet broth over low heat until just warm. Whisk in the flour to form a smooth paste. Slowly add the flour mixture to the broth in the Dutch oven, stirring well. Cook slowly, stirring constantly, for about 5 minutes, until blended and gravy thickens.

Combine the milk and water in a small bowl and gradually add to the gravy mixture, beating constantly with a whisk until smooth. If the gravy is too thick, add more water or milk to reach the desired consistency. Add the salt and white pepper. Keep warm.

CORN OYSTERS

SERVES 4 TO 6

We didn't make a mistake—there's not an oyster anywhere in this recipe. The name came from the similarity of the fried corncakes to oysters fried in cornmeal batter. Both are good!

Corn oil

1 cup freshly grated corn, drained

1 tablespoon all-purpose flour

1 tablespoon salted butter, melted

1 large egg

1 teaspoon salt

Line a plate with paper towels. Heat 1/8 inch of corn oil in a sauté pan over medium-high heat. In a medium bowl, combine all the ingredients. Drop the batter by tablespoonsful into the hot oil and fry, turning once, until golden brown. Transfer to the plate and sprinkle with additional salt. Serve immediately.

CREAMED FRESH CORN

SERVES 4 TO 6

6 ears fresh white corn, shucked and
  silks removed
8 tablespoons (1 stick) salted butter, or
  1/2 cup bacon drippings

1 teaspoon salt
1/8 teaspoon white pepper
1 1/2 teaspoons sugar (optional)
1/4 cup warm whole milk (optional)

Working over a large bowl, with a very sharp knife, cut off the top one-third tips of the
corn kernels on each cob. Repeat the procedure twice. Scrape the milk from the cobs into
the bowl.

In a large, heavy skillet, melt the butter or drippings over medium heat. Add the corn
with juices to the skillet. Stir in the salt and white pepper. Bring to a simmer; cover and
cook for about 10 minutes, until the corn is tender. If the corn seems a bit dry, you may
stir in a enough whole milk to soften the mixture.

EGGPLANT CASSEROLE

SERVES 4 TO 6

I medium eggplant, peeled and diced

I cup soda cracker crumbs

2 large eggs

I cup diced celery

1/2 cup minced sweet onion

3 tablespoons salted butter, melted

I teaspoon salt

1/4 teaspoon freshly ground black pepper

1/2 cup Cheddar cheese

Preheat the oven to 350°F. Butter a 2-quart casserole dish. In a saucepan over medium heat, cook the eggplant in salted water to cover for about 15 minutes, or until the eggplant is tender. Drain well and place in a bowl. Add the cracker crumbs and the remaining ingredients, reserving a little cheese and cracker crumbs for the topping, and mix well. Pour into the casserole dish, top with the reserved cheese and cracker crumbs, and bake for 40 minutes, or until bubbly and golden brown.

CITY CHEESE GRITS

SERVES 6

3 cups water

1 cup quick-cooking grits

1 1/4 cups heavy cream or whole milk

1/2 teaspoon salt

1/2 cup crumbled Stilton blue cheese, or
   4 ounces Saga blue cheese

In a large saucepan, bring the water to a simmer; whisk in the grits. Cook for 8 minutes, whisking frequently. Add the heavy cream or milk, 1/4 cup at a time, whisking until each addition is combined. Cook for 10 minutes, stirring frequently. Add the salt and the cheese, stirring until the cheese is melted.

COUNTRY CHEESE GRITS

SERVES 6

The difference is the type of cheese, of course. Any old cheese will do for this version.

3 cups water

1 cup quick-cooking grits

1 1/4 cups heavy cream or whole milk

1/2 teaspoon salt

1 cup shredded sharp Cheddar cheese

In a large saucepan, bring the water to a simmer; whisk in the grits. Cook for 8 minutes, whisking frequently. Add the heavy cream or milk, 1/4 cup at a time, whisking until each addition is combined. Cook for 10 minutes, stirring frequently. Add the salt and the cheese, stirring until the cheese is melted.

WHIPPED POTATOES

SERVES 6 TO 8

3 1/2 pounds russet potatoes, peeled
  and cubed

4 cups water

1 teaspoon salt

8 tablespoons (1 stick) salted butter,
  softened

1/2 cup to 1 cup warm whole milk

1/2 teaspoon white pepper

Salt and freshly ground black pepper

In a large stockpot, combine the potatoes, water, and salt and bring to a boil over medium-high heat. Reduce the heat to low, cover, and cook for 15 minutes, or until the potatoes are fork-tender. Drain the potatoes; place in the work bowl of a stand mixer. With the whisk attachment, on low speed, beat until no lumps remain; add the butter, the 1/2 cup of milk, and the white pepper and blend well. Add more milk to reach the desired consistency. Add salt and black pepper to taste.

ZUCCHINI FRENCH FRIES

SERVES 4 TO 6

2 cups vegetable oil

3 large zucchini, peeled

1 cup all-purpose flour

Salt

Heat the oil in a deep-fryer or heavy deep skillet to 375°F. Cut the zucchini into 3 by 1/2-inch strips. Place the flour in a shallow bowl; dredge the strips in the flour. Fry the zucchini until lightly browned. Drain on paper towels and sprinkle with salt. Serve with ketchup.

MACARONI AND CHEESE

SERVES 4 TO 6

Flora has cooked our mac and cheese for thirty-five years. Her dish is the gold standard for this classic crowd-pleaser.

3 large eggs

2 cups evaporated milk

1/2 teaspoon salt

1/2 teaspoon white pepper

I teaspoon sugar

2 tablespoons salted butter, melted

I teaspoon hot sauce

1/2 pound elbow macaroni, cooked according to package directions and drained

2 cups shredded extra-sharp Cheddar cheese

1/4 teaspoon sweet paprika

Preheat the oven to 350°F. Butter an 8 by 8-inch baking dish. In a large bowl, whisk the eggs until light yellow. Add the evaporated milk, salt, white pepper, sugar, melted butter, and hot sauce. Layer half of the macaroni, half of the milk mixture, and half of the cheese in the baking dish. Repeat the procedure, ending with the cheese. Sprinkle the paprika over the cheese; bake for 35 to 40 minutes, until set.

OKRA AND TOMATOES

SERVES 4 TO 6

1 (14 1/2-ounce) can crushed tomatoes, undrained

1 teaspoon salt

1/2 teaspoon white pepper

1 tablespoon sugar

2 tablespoons salted butter, melted, or strained bacon drippings

1/2 pound okra, stemmed and cut into 1/4-inch slices

2 teaspoons cornstarch (optional)

2 teaspoons cold water (optional)

In a heavy saucepan, combine the tomatoes, salt, white pepper, sugar, and melted butter or bacon drippings. Cook over medium-high heat for 10 minutes. Add the okra, reduce the heat, and simmer for 5 minutes. (To thicken the stew, mix together the cornstarch and cold water in a small bowl until smooth. Add to the stew and bring to a boil, stirring until thickened to the desired consistency.) Add additional salt and white pepper to taste.

Favorite Diners

The Georgia Tech Guys

For the past thirty years, a group of professors from nearby Georgia Tech College has met for lunch at Mary Mac's. Bill Sayle, now deceased, was the official leader of the Georgia Tech lunchtime group and his picture now hangs on the wall near their regular table. Paul Steffes recently told me, "You saved the restaurant, John. It just wouldn't have made it without you." On the contrary, Paul, we wouldn't have made it without people like you and the Georgia Tech guys!

PICKLED BEETS

SERVES 4 TO 6

1 pound whole beets

1/2 cup sugar

1 cup cider vinegar

1 1/2 teaspoons mustard seed

3/4 teaspoon celery seed

1 1/2 teaspoons salt

In a heavy pot, bring the beets and enough water to cover to a boil. Cover and reduce the heat to a simmer, cooking for about 45 minutes, or until the beets are tender. (Larger beets may take up to 1 hour.) Drain the beets and let cool. Peel and cut the beets into 1/4-inch slices and place in a large bowl.

In a heavy saucepan, combine the sugar, vinegar, mustard seed, celery seed, and salt and bring to a boil over medium-high heat. Pour over the beets; let cool. Chill for 2 to 3 hours before serving.

TOMATO GRAVY OVER RICE

SERVES 4 TO 6

Any fresh vegetable, such as corn or bell pepper, can be added to the tomatoes in this recipe.

6 strips lean bacon

1 large sweet onion, chopped

2 (14 1/2-ounce) cans diced tomatoes, undrained

1 cup sliced fresh or frozen okra

1 teaspoon sugar

1/4 teaspoon salt

1/2 teaspoon freshly ground black pepper

3 cups hot cooked rice

In a heavy skillet over medium heat, cook the bacon until crisp. Transfer to paper towels to drain, reserving the drippings in the skillet. When cool enough to handle, crumble the bacon and set aside. Sauté the onion in the drippings for 2 to 3 minutes over medium heat. Add the canned tomatoes and the okra to the pan and cook over medium heat, stirring occasionally, for about 15 minutes, or until thickened. Add the sugar, salt, and pepper, stirring to combine. Serve the tomatoes over the rice; sprinkle the crumbled bacon on top.

POTATO CAKES

SERVES 4 TO 6

3 cups mashed potatoes

1 cup finely chopped yellow onion

1 tablespoon buttermilk powder

1/2 teaspoon dried parsley

1/8 teaspoon dried dill

1/2 teaspoon onion powder

1/8 teaspoon garlic powder

1/2 teaspoon salt

1/8 teaspoon white pepper

2 large eggs, lightly beaten

1/2 cup buttermilk

1 cup all-purpose flour

Canola oil

In a large bowl, combine the mashed potatoes, onion, buttermilk powder, seasonings, eggs, and buttermilk. Add the flour and stir until blended.

In a sauté pan over medium heat, heat enough canola oil to just cover the bottom of the pan. Place 1/3 cup of the potato mixture in the pan, flattening gently with a spatula. Sauté 2 to 4 cakes at a time, cooking on each side for about 3 minutes, or until golden. Repeat the procedure, adding the canola oil as needed for subsequent batches. Serve immediately.

SQUASH SOUFFLÉ

SERVES 6 TO 8

1/2 cup water

1 3/4 teaspoons salt

2 pounds yellow summer squash, sliced into 1/4-inch rounds

4 tablespoons (1/2 stick) salted butter

2 large eggs

1 cup whole milk

1/2 teaspoon white pepper

1 tablespoon salted butter, melted

1/2 cup bread crumbs

1/2 cup shredded Cheddar cheese

Preheat the oven to 350°F. Lightly grease a 2-quart baking dish. In a saucepan, combine the water and 1 teaspoon of the salt and bring to a boil over medium-high heat. Add the squash; reduce the heat to a simmer, and cook, covered, for 15 minutes. Remove the pan from the heat; add the butter and mash the squash with a potato masher to desired consistency.

In a large bowl, beat the eggs; add the milk, the remaining 3/4 teaspoon salt, the white pepper, and the melted butter, mixing well. Add the squash mixture, stirring to combine. Pour into the baking dish and top with the bread crumbs and cheese. Bake for 40 to 50 minutes, until the soufflé is set in the center.

SUNDAY SQUASH CASSEROLE

This recipe was given to me by my cousin, David Stringer, of Springhill, Georgia. When you serve this dish, ask your guests to guess at what the main ingredient is. The taste is delightful, but it is not instantly recognizable as squash.

1/2 cup water

2 pounds yellow summer squash, sliced into 1/4-inch rounds

3 large eggs

1 cup whole milk

8 tablespoons (1 stick) salted butter, melted

1/2 cup sugar

1/2 teaspoon ground ginger

2 tablespoons sweetened flaked coconut, or 1/2 teaspoon coconut extract

24 Ritz crackers, crushed

Preheat the oven to 350°F. Butter a 2-quart casserole dish. In a saucepan, bring the water to a boil over medium-high heat; add the squash. Reduce the heat to a simmer and cook, covered, for 15 minutes. Remove from the heat and mash the squash with a potato masher to the desired consistency.

In a large bowl, beat the eggs; add the milk, 6 tablespoons of the melted butter, the sugar, ginger, and coconut, mixing well. Add the mashed squash, stirring to combine. Pour into the casserole dish and place the casserole dish into a larger baking dish; place the pans in the oven. Pour boiling water into the outer dish until it comes about halfway up the sides of the casserole dish. Bake for 45 minutes.

Mix together the cracker crumbs and the remaining 2 tablespoons melted butter. Remove the casserole from the oven and top with the crumb mixture; bake for 5 minutes, or until golden brown.

SWEET POTATO SOUFFLÉ

SERVES 4 TO 6

The sugar content of sweet potatoes varies according to season and where they are grown, so be sure to taste the mixture before adding the sugar to adjust the level of sweetness to your liking. Try our variation with raisins and pecans, if you don't like the marshmallows.

1 pound small sweet potatoes
4 tablespoons (1/2 stick) salted butter, softened
5 to 6 tablespoons sugar
Pinch of ground cinnamon

Pinch of ground nutmeg
1 teaspoon pure vanilla extract
1/3 cup light cream
2 large eggs, lightly beaten
2 cups miniature marshmallows

Preheat the oven to 350°F. Butter a 2-quart baking dish. Place the sweet potatoes in a large stockpot with water to cover. Bring to a boil over medium-high heat; reduce the heat, cover, and simmer for about 1 hour, or until soft. Drain and let cool. Remove the skins and mash the sweet potatoes well with a potato masher in a large bowl.

Add the butter, sugar, cinnamon, nutmeg, vanilla, and cream to the mashed sweet potatoes, stirring to combine. Taste for sweetness and adjust the sugar as desired. Add the beaten eggs, stirring to combine. Pour into the baking dish and bake for 30 to 40 minutes, until the soufflé is set in the center.

Increase the oven temperature to 475°F. Cover the top of the soufflé with the miniature marshmallows and bake for 4 to 5 minutes, until the marshmallows are browned.

VARIATION: Omit the cinnamon, nutmeg, and marshmallows and fold in 1/2 cup of raisins and/or 1/2 cup of chopped pecans.

TURNIP SOUFFLÉ

SERVES 4 TO 6

"As God is my witness, I'll never be hungry again." Those were Scarlett O'Hara's words as she pulled a lowly turnip out of the ground of her war-ravaged plantation. The scrappy heroine would be proud of this tasty Southern recipe that glorifies her crop!

2 pounds turnips, peeled, quartered, and thinly sliced

1 medium sweet onion, halved and thinly sliced

1/2 teaspoon salt

3 cups water

1 1/2 tablespoons salted butter

1 1/2 tablespoons all-purpose flour

1 1/2 cups whole milk

3 large eggs, lightly beaten

4 tablespoons (1/2 stick) salted butter, melted

1 teaspoon sugar

1/2 teaspoon white pepper

1 sleeve (1/4 pound) Ritz crackers, crushed

2 tablespoons salted butter, cut into small pieces

In a medium saucepan, place the turnips, onion, and salt in the 3 cups water and bring to a boil over medium-high heat. Boil for 5 minutes. Reduce the heat to medium; cover and cook for 45 minutes, or until tender. Drain; place the turnip mixture in a bowl, and mash with a potato masher to the desired consistency.

Preheat the oven to 350°F. Butter a 12 by 8-inch casserole dish. In a large sauté pan over medium heat, melt 1 1/2 tablespoons butter; whisk in the flour. Cook for 2 minutes, or until foamy. Slowly whisk in the milk until the mixture is smooth. Bring to a boil, stirring until thickened; remove from the heat and let cool.

In a medium bowl, combine the beaten eggs, the 4 tablespoons melted butter, the sugar, and the white pepper. Add the milk mixture and the mashed turnip mixture, stirring to combine. Pour into the casserole dish. Sprinkle the cracker crumbs over the mixture and dot with the 2 tablespoons butter. Bake for 25 to 30 minutes, until the top of the soufflé is golden brown.

DESSERTS

❖

Plus a few kind words,

kudos, and awards that

we've garnered over

the decades

❖

KUDOS

ALTHOUGH OUR BUSINESS THRIVES because of our loyal customers, dedicated staff, and hard work, none of this would matter if Mary Mac's didn't serve good food. We are proud of the countless good reviews and awards that the restaurant has received over six decades, and strive daily to keep the tradition of good-quality "meat and three" cooking alive in the South.

For those who have never heard the term "meat and three," it refers to the choice of any meat and three vegetable side dishes, served fresh daily by a nonchain cafe, restaurant, or diner. By strict definition, the menu is set and remains the same (with a few daily specials), and in some places it is even affixed to the wall. You'll see some of our old menus in this book, and while we have made changes and additions to update the menu, the basics of Southern fare remain the same.

While similar to a blue plate special, that particular meal deviates from the "meat and three" menu to be anything the management desires to serve, and can change daily or weekly. The fundamental philosophy is to provide fresh, local food at reasonable prices to all types of clientele—blue-collar workers, businessmen, professionals, politicians, and families. The tradition of "meat and three" restaurants is slowly dying, pushed out of business by chains and more upscale eateries, and there are only a few left in Atlanta—Mary Mac's being the most famous and enduring. When I say that we strive to uphold traditions at Mary Mac's, I am very cognizant of the historic significance of keeping this style of restaurant food alive.

Luckily, we have garnered great reviews and kudos from writers, newspapers, and magazines throughout the years. We proudly display all awards, to let our diners see that the quality of Mary Mac's food is recognized and constant. If we read a bad review, we take pains to correct any mistakes that have been pointed out.

Usually, a review of Mary Mac's food will note the "pot likker" on the menu, because it is one of the things that is so hard to find on

Southern menus these days. I don't know why that is, because it is a staple of the food I grew up with and is instantly recognizable to anyone who knows their way around a Southern kitchen. But it is what we are known best for—that and our fried chicken.

Atlanta's own Nathalie Dupree, who hosted a weekly public television cooking show in the '80s, spoke in an article in the *Chicago Tribune* (October 1987) about the resurgence of Southern cooking: "Southern food (however prepared) has the flavors people crave, as opposed to this whole era of contrived foods; an arugula leaf just is never going to be as satisfying as a mess of greens."

We have been pleased to be included regularly in many "best of" dining guides, and have been described by *Gourmet* magazine (October 2000) as "a midtown Atlanta institution that has been proving the existence of Southern gentility for 55 years."

Fodor's review is on the money about Mary Mac's with this bit of information: "Local celebrities and ordinary folks line up for the country-fried steak, fried chicken, and fresh vegetables. Here, in the Southern tradition, waitresses will call you 'honey' and pat your arm to assure you that everything's all right. It's a great way to experience Southern food and hospitality all at once."

Kelly Alexander, writing for *Saveur* magazine about Atlanta's food scene in 2003, names Mary Mac's a destination for "finger-lickin' good, real Southern food." And the *Atlanta Journal-Constitution* and *Creative Loafing* magazine consistently give Mary Mac's their top awards for Best Southern Food and Best Soul Food.

Of course, awards are wonderful and the importance of having that spotlight on your business cannot be overlooked. Good reviews translate into good business. But I've always said that it's the opinions of our customers that really keep our business healthy year-in and year-out. The many personal letters and notes I receive from both loyal customers and first-time visitors find their way onto our "walls of fame" along with the awards and reviews. Each room of the restaurant is decorated with this part of our history, and there is no artwork I'd rather look at than these framed memories of the people we've served.

I invite you to visit Mary Mac's the next time you're in Atlanta, and I hope that you enjoy these recipes from our kitchen and our heart. They are family-friendly and sure crowd pleasers, and I'm happy to be able to share sixty-five years of good food with you.

"Here, in the Southern tradition, waitresses will call you 'honey' and pat your arm to assure you that everything's all right. It's a great way to experience Southern food and hospitality all at once."

—FODOR'S review

OPPOSITE, CLOCKWISE FROM TOP: DOORWAYS TO TWO OF OUR SEVEN DINING ROOMS, THE PONCE AND THE BOARD ROOM; THE ENTRANCE TO MARY MAC'S, WHERE YOU WILL BE GREETED LIKE FAMILY.

BLACKBERRY JAM CAKE

SERVES 12 TO 14

2/3 cup shortening

2 cups sugar

4 large eggs

3 cups sifted all-purpose flour

2 tablespoons cocoa powder

1/2 teaspoon salt

1 teaspoon baking soda

1/2 teaspoon ground nutmeg

1 teaspoon ground allspice

1 teaspoon ground cloves

2 teaspoons ground cinnamon

2/3 cup buttermilk

1 cup seedless blackberry jam

1 cup applesauce

Caramel Icing (recipe follows)

Preheat the oven to 350°F. Grease and flour 3 (9-inch) cake pans.

In the work bowl of a stand mixer, combine the shortening and 1 cup of the sugar. With the whisk attachment, on medium speed, beat until light and fluffy. Add the eggs, one at a time, beating after each addition. In a large bowl, sift together the flour, the remaining 1 cup sugar, the cocoa powder, salt, baking soda, and spices three times. Add the dry ingredients to the shortening, alternately with the buttermilk mixture. Stir in the jam and applesauce. Divide the batter among the 3 pans and bake for 30 to 40 minutes, until a tester inserted in the center of the cake comes out clean. Let the cake cool in the pans for 10 minutes. Remove from the pans, and let cool completely on wire racks. Spread the caramel icing between the layers and on the top and the sides of the cake.

CARAMEL ICING

1 1/2 cups firmly packed brown sugar

1/3 cup cream or evaporated milk

8 tablespoons (1 stick) salted butter

1 1/2 cups confectioners' sugar

Combine the brown sugar, cream, and butter in a heavy saucepan over medium heat. Bring to a boil; cook for 2 minutes, stirring constantly. Remove from the heat and add the confectioners' sugar. Using an electric hand mixer, beat at medium speed until smooth. Use immediately to frost the cake so the icing doesn't stiffen or harden.

APPLESAUCE CAKE

SERVES 10 TO 12

1½ cups applesauce

2 teaspoons baking soda

1 cup sugar

½ cup cocoa powder

1 teaspoon ground cloves

1 teaspoon ground cinnamon

1 teaspoon ground nutmeg

8 tablespoons (1 stick) salted butter, melted

2 cups self-rising flour

½ cup raisins

½ cup chopped walnuts or pecans (optional)

Preheat the oven to 350°F. Butter or grease and flour a 10-inch tube pan. In the work bowl of a stand mixer with the whisk attachment, on medium speed, mix the applesauce with the baking soda. Add the sugar, cocoa powder, spices, and melted butter. Add the flour, raisins, and nuts. Pour the batter into the pan. Bake for 45 minutes, or until a tester inserted near the center of the cake comes out clean. Let cool in the pan for 10 minutes; remove the cake from the pan and let cool completely on a wire rack.

Favorite Diners

Hillary Clinton

On May 2, 1995, First Lady Hillary Rodham Clinton dropped in at Mary Mac's with her large entourage for a scheduled roundtable discussion with working women. She was served a working lunch of "to go" fried chicken, sweet potatoes, sweet tea, and pound cake. Mrs. Clinton seemed to enjoy herself while discussing women's and children's issues.

A year later, during the 1996 Olympic Games, daughter Chelsea Clinton stopped by Mary Mac's. She told me her mother had recommended it for some good food.

BUTTERNUT CAKE

MAKES 1 (8-INCH) CAKE

This is a cake to remember, and easy to make, provided you can find the butternut extract. We found it at J.R.Watkins Naturals, www.watkinsonline.com.

2 cups sugar

1 cup shortening

4 large eggs

2 cups self-rising flour

1 cup whole milk

1 tablespoon butternut flavoring

Butternut Cream Cheese Frosting
  (recipe follows)

Preheat the oven to 350°F. Grease and flour 3 (8-inch) cake pans.

In the work bowl of a stand mixer with the whisk attachment, on medium speed, beat the sugar and shortening until light and fluffy. Add the eggs, one at a time, beating well after each addition. Add 1/2 cup flour alternately with 1/4 cup milk, beating well after each addition. Repeat the process four times, until the flour and milk are combined. Stir in the butternut flavoring. Divide the batter among the 3 cake pans and bake for 20 minutes, or until a tester inserted into the center of the cake comes out clean.

Let the cake layers cool completely in the pans. Remove from the pans and let cool on wire racks. Spread the frosting between the layers and on the top and sides of the cake.

BUTTERNUT CREAM CHEESE FROSTING

3 (3-ounce) packages cream cheese,
  softened

1 tablespoon butternut flavoring

2 (16-ounce) boxes confectioners' sugar

2 to 3 tablespoons water

1/2 to 1 cup pecans, toasted and chopped

In the work bowl of a stand mixer, place the cream cheese and add the butternut flavoring. With the whisk attachment, on medium speed, add the confectioners' sugar gradually, beating until well blended. Add the 2 tablespoons water as needed to reach the desired consistency. Add the third tablespoon, if necessary. Gently stir in the pecans.

BREAD PUDDING WITH WINE SAUCE

SERVES 6 TO 8

10 slices white bread, crusts removed

1 1/2 cups whole milk

3 large eggs

3/4 cup sugar

1 tablespoon baking powder

Pinch of salt

3 tablespoons unsalted butter, melted

2 cups fresh fruit, such as apples, peaches, or cherries, sweetened and drained

Wine Sauce (recipe follows)

Preheat the oven to 325°F. Butter a 2-quart baking dish. In a medium bowl, soak the bread in the milk for 5 minutes. In the work bowl of a stand mixer with the whisk attachment, on medium speed, beat the eggs until light in color. Stir in the bread mixture, sugar, baking powder, pinch of salt, melted butter, and fruit. Mix together well and pour into baking dish. Bake for 30 minutes, or until a knife inserted in the center comes out clean. Serve with wine sauce. Serve hot.

WINE SAUCE

1/2 pound (2 sticks) unsalted butter

2 cups red wine

2 1/2 cups firmly packed brown sugar

2 large eggs, lightly beaten

Place the butter, wine, and brown sugar in the top of a double boiler and melt, stirring often with a whisk. Bring almost to a boil over medium-high heat, until small bubbles appear around the edges. Slowly add the eggs to the wine mixture, beating constantly. Continue beating as the mixture thickens over the heat. When all the foam disappears, remove the top part of the double boiler from the heat and beat the sauce quickly and thoroughly with the whisk. The sauce should be as smooth as syrup. Serve the sauce hot or store in the refrigerator or freezer for up to 1 month. When reheating, add red wine for flavor.

BANANA CREAM PIE

SERVES 8

1/2 cup firmly packed light brown sugar

1/2 cup granulated sugar

1/3 cup cornstarch

1/4 teaspoon salt

2 1/2 cups heavy cream

1 1/2 cups whole milk

3 large egg yolks

2 tablespoons (1/4 stick) unsalted butter, softened

2 1/2 teaspoons pure vanilla extract

3 medium bananas

1 (9-inch) pie shell, prebaked

1 teaspoon freshly squeezed lemon juice

In a large saucepan, mix together the brown sugar, 1/4 cup of the granulated sugar, the cornstarch, and salt. Whisk in 1 1/2 cups of the heavy cream, the whole milk, and egg yolks. Place the saucepan over medium heat and slowly bring to a boil, stirring with a wooden spoon. When the custard thickens, remove from the heat. Add the softened butter and 1 1/2 teaspoons of the vanilla and stir well to blend. Slice 2 of the bananas and place in the bottom of the pie crust; pour the custard over the bananas, spreading evenly. Chill the pie for 3 to 4 hours, until the custard is firm.

In the bowl of a stand mixer with the whisk attachment, on medium-high speed, beat the remaining 1 cup heavy cream and 1/2 teaspoon vanilla until soft peaks form. Gradually add the remaining 1/4 cup granulated sugar and beat until stiff peaks form. Spread the sweetened whipped cream over the chilled pie.

Slice the remaining banana and dip each slice in the lemon juice to prevent browning. Place the banana slices decoratively around the edges of the whipped cream.

BANANA PUDDING

For years this has been the most popular dessert at Mary Mac's. Once I was at a restaurant in Montana and a large group was seated next to me. I overheard a woman exclaim, "I sure could go for some Mary Mac's banana pudding right now!"

3/4 cup granulated sugar

1/3 cup all-purpose flour

1/8 teaspoon salt

3 large eggs, separated

2 cups whole milk

1/2 teaspoon pure vanilla extract

1 (12-ounce) package vanilla wafers

6 medium bananas, thinly sliced

Preheat the oven to 350°F. Butter a 9 by 9-inch square baking dish. In a large bowl, combine 1/2 cup of the sugar, the flour, salt, egg yolks, and milk. Place the bowl over a medium saucepan of simmering water or in the top of a double boiler. Cook, uncovered, stirring constantly, for 10 to 12 minutes, until thickened. Remove from the heat and stir in the vanilla.

Pour 1/2 cup of the custard into the bottom of the baking dish. Arrange one-third of the wafers over the custard. Arrange one-third of the sliced bananas over the wafers. Pour one-third of the remaining custard over the bananas. Repeat the layers twice, ending with custard on top.

In the work bowl of a stand mixer, beat the egg whites until soft peaks form. Add the remaining 1/4 cup sugar, 1 tablespoon at a time, beating until stiff peaks form. Spread the meringue evenly over the top of the pie, from edge to edge. Bake for 12 to 15 minutes, until lightly browned. Let cool for 20 minutes before serving.

BLACKBERRY SONKER

SERVES 6 TO 8

There are many opinions about what constitutes a "sonker." Other names for the dish include buckle, betty, and cobbler. They are all variations on a fruit-and-dough dessert theme.

3 pints fresh blackberries, washed and drained, with a little water clinging to the fruit

1 1/2 cups sugar plus additional for sprinkling

1 1/2 tablespoons cornstarch

1 1/2 tablespoons all-purpose flour

Biscuit Dough (recipe follows)

2 tablespoons (1/4 stick) unsalted butter, cut into small pieces

Preheat the oven to 400°F. Grease a 2-quart baking dish. Gently combine the blackberries with 1 1/2 cups sugar, the cornstarch, and flour in a medium bowl and pour into the baking dish. Pat the dough on a floured surface into a 9-inch round of about 1/4 inch thickness. The size and shape may be adjusted to suit your baking dish. Place the dough on top of the berry mixture and tuck in the edges. Make 3 or 4 slits in the pastry with a sharp knife for steam to escape. Dot the top of the pastry with the butter. Sprinkle the top with a little sugar. Bake for 10 minutes, then reduce the oven temperature to 300°F and continue baking for another 20 to 25 minutes, until the filling bubbles around the edges and through the slits in the pastry. Serve warm with vanilla ice cream or whipped cream.

BISCUIT DOUGH

2 cups all-purpose flour

1 tablespoon baking powder

1 teaspoon salt

8 tablespoons (1 stick) unsalted butter

3/4 cup whole milk

In a mixing bowl, combine the flour, baking powder, and salt. Cut in the butter with your fingers or 2 forks until the mixture resembles coarse cornmeal. Add the milk and stir in with a fork just until the dry ingredients are moistened. Turn out onto a floured surface and knead the dough together gently before rolling and cutting into rounds.

BUTTERMILK PIE

SERVES 8 TO 10

1 1/2 cups sugar

8 tablespoons (1 stick) salted butter, softened

3 tablespoons all-purpose flour

3 large eggs

1/2 teaspoon pure vanilla extract or lemon extract

1/2 cup buttermilk

1 (9-inch) deep-dish pie shell, unbaked

Preheat the oven to 400°F. In the work bowl of a stand mixer with the whisk attachment on medium speed, beat the sugar and butter until light and fluffy. Add the flour and mix well. Add the eggs, one at a time, beating well after each addition. Add the vanilla or lemon extract and buttermilk and mix well. Pour the filling into the unbaked pie shell. Bake for 10 minutes, then reduce the oven temperature to 325°F and bake for 25 to 30 minutes, until a tester inserted in the center comes out clean.

SWEET POTATO PIE

MAKES 2 (9-INCH) PIES, SERVES 16 TO 20

2 pounds medium sweet potatoes, unpeeled

4 cups water

4 medium eggs, lightly beaten

1 tablespoon pure vanilla extract

1 tablespoon ground nutmeg

1 teaspoon ground cinnamon

2 cups sugar

1 cup evaporated milk

12 tablespoons (1 1/2 sticks) salted butter, melted

2 (9-inch) pie shells, unbaked

Preheat the oven to 350°F. Place the sweet potatoes and the water in a large saucepan. Cook over medium-high heat for 45 to 60 minutes until you can stick a fork through the potatoes, and they are soft. Drain, peel the potatoes under cold running water, and place in a bowl. Whisk the potatoes until smooth. Add the eggs, vanilla, nutmeg, cinnamon, sugar, evaporated milk, and melted butter and beat thoroughly. Divide the sweet potato mixture evenly between the 2 pie shells. Bake for 50 to 60 minutes. Remove from the oven when a knife inserted into the middle of the pies comes out clean. Let cool on a rack for 20 to 25 minutes before serving.

GEORGIA PEACH COBBLER

SERVES 8 TO 10

2 pounds fresh fruit or 1 (16-ounce)
   can sliced peaches in heavy syrup,
   undrained
1 cup plus 3/4 teaspoon sugar
1 teaspoon freshly squeezed lemon juice
1/4 teaspoon ground cinnamon
1/8 teaspoon ground nutmeg
1 teaspoon pure vanilla extract
2 teaspoons cornstarch

8 tablespoons (1 stick) salted butter,
   cut into small pieces
1/2 cup shortening
3/4 teaspoon salt
1 3/4 cups all-purpose flour
1/3 cup ice water (with crushed ice)
2 tablespoons (1/4 stick) unsalted
   butter, melted

Preheat the oven to 350°F. Peel and slice the fresh fruit. (If using canned fruit, taste before adding the sugar.) Place the fruit in a bowl and add 1 cup of the sugar, lemon juice, cinnamon, nutmeg, vanilla, and cornstarch. Toss together gently. Pour the sweetened fruit into a 13 by 9-inch baking dish and dot with the butter pieces.

In the work bowl of a stand mixer with the paddle attachment, on medium speed, beat the shortening, salt, and the remaining 3/4 teaspoon sugar. Gradually add 1/2 cup of the flour to the shortening mixture and mix together lightly. When the mixture becomes stiff, add 1 tablespoon of the ice water. Repeat the process until all the flour and water is used. The mixture should be soft, but not wet. Cover and let chill for 30 to 40 minutes. Roll out on a floured surface to a 13 by 9 1/2-inch rectangle.

Cover the fruit with the pastry, crimping the edges. Make 3 or 4 slits in the pastry with a sharp knife for steam to escape. Brush the crust with the 2 tablespoons of melted butter. If using fresh fruit, cook for 1 hour. If using canned fruit, cook for 25 to 30 minutes at 400°F. The cobbler is done when the pastry is golden. Serve warm with vanilla ice cream or whipped cream.

FRUIT CAKE

SERVES 12 TO 16

This special cake takes several weeks to mature. Start it 2 to 3 weeks before the holidays. My mother's version allowed for a half-jigger of whiskey poured all around the top of the cake every 3 to 4 days until served.

1 pound (4 sticks) unsalted butter, softened

2 cups sugar

6 large eggs, lightly beaten

2 teaspoons pure vanilla extract

4 cups all-purpose flour

1 tablespoon baking powder

1/4 teaspoon salt

1/2 pound candied pineapple

1/2 pound candied cherries

4 cups chopped pecans, toasted

Bourbon

1 medium apple

Preheat the oven to 250°F. Butter and flour a 10-inch tube pan. In the work bowl of a stand mixer with the whisk attachment, on medium speed, beat the butter and sugar until light and fluffy. Add the eggs one at a time, beating well to combine. Stir in the vanilla. Sift together 3 cups of the flour, the baking powder, and salt; add to batter, beating until combined.

Toss the remaining 1 cup flour with the pineapple, cherries, and pecans in a medium bowl and add to the batter, mixing well. Pour the batter into the tube pan and bake for 3 hours. Turn the oven off and leave the cake in the oven overnight.

Remove the cake from the pan and wrap it in cheesecloth. Place the wrapped cake inside a large baking pan and pour a jigger of bourbon over the cake. Cut the apple into quarters and place inside the pan next to the cake to keep it moist. Let the cake stand for a week. Pour another jigger of bourbon over it. You may let it stand for a third week, adding more bourbon, as desired.

CARAMEL CREAM CAKE

SERVES 16

1/2 pound (2 sticks) unsalted butter,
  softened

2 1/2 cups sugar

5 large eggs, separated

3 cups all-purpose flour

1 teaspoon baking soda

1 teaspoon salt

4 teaspoons cocoa powder

1 cup buttermilk

5 teaspoons strong coffee

2 teaspoons pure vanilla extract

Caramel Cream Frosting (recipe follows)

Preheat the oven to 350°F. Butter and flour the bottom and sides of 3 (9-inch) round cake pans.

In the work bowl of a stand mixer with the whisk attachment, on medium speed, beat the butter until light and fluffy. Add the sugar and egg yolks and beat until well combined. Sift together the dry ingredients and add to the butter mixture alternately with the buttermilk, beginning and ending with the dry ingredients. Add the coffee and vanilla and beat well. In a clean bowl using clean beaters, beat the egg whites until stiff peaks form; gently fold into the batter.

Divide the batter among the 3 pans and bake for 30 minutes, or until a tester inserted into the center of the cake comes out clean.

Let the cake cool in the pans on wire racks for 10 minutes; remove from the pans and let cool completely on the racks. Spread the frosting in between the layers and on the top.

CARAMEL CREAM FROSTING

1 (16-ounce) box confectioners' sugar

2 teaspoons cocoa powder

1 egg yolk

8 tablespoons (1 stick) unsalted butter,
  softened

1 tablespoon strong coffee, (liquid, not
  grounds)

1 teaspoon pure vanilla extract

Sift together the confectioners' sugar and cocoa powder. In the work bowl of a stand mixer with the whisk attachment, on low speed, beat the egg yolk until pale. Add the butter and beat well. Add the liquids, beating until light and fluffy.

NOTE: *This recipe contains uncooked egg. This may be a health concern for the very young, the elderly, pregnant women, and those with weak immune systems.*

BIG OLD-FASHIONED SUGAR COOKIES

MAKES ABOUT A DOZEN LARGE COOKIES

3 1/4 cups all-purpose flour

1 teaspoon baking soda

1/2 teaspoon salt

8 tablespoons (1 stick) salted butter, softened

1 cup sugar plus additional for sprinkling

1 large egg

1 teaspoon pure vanilla extract

1/2 cup sour cream

Lightly grease 2 baking sheets. Sift together the flour, baking soda, and salt. In the work bowl of a stand mixer with the whisk attachment, on medium speed, beat the butter and sugar until fluffy. Add the egg and vanilla, beating at medium-high speed for 2 minutes. Reduce the speed to low and add the dry ingredients and sour cream, beating well. Chill the dough for 1 hour.

Preheat the oven to 400°F. On a generously floured surface, roll the dough out to 1/4 inch thick. Cut with a 4-inch round cookie cutter dipped in flour and place 1/2 inch apart on the baking sheets. (The dough is very soft; if it gets too sticky, refrigerate to chill between batches.) Sprinkle the cookies with sugar. Bake for 7 to 9 minutes, until firm and lightly browned on the bottoms.

COCONUT CREAM PIE

SERVES 8

1 1/4 cups sugar

1/4 cup cornstarch

1/4 teaspoon salt

2 cups whole milk

3 large eggs, separated

2 tablespoons (1/4 stick) salted butter,
    softened

1 (3 1/2-ounce) can flaked coconut

1 1/2 teaspoon coconut extract

1/2 teaspoon pure vanilla extract

1/4 teaspoon cream of tartar

1 (9-inch) pie shell, prebaked

Combine the sugar, cornstarch, and salt in the top of a double boiler. Blend in the whole milk, using a whisk. Heat the water in the double boiler to boiling, stirring the milk mixture constantly until it thickens, about 25 minutes.

In a separate bowl, beat the egg yolks until thick and lemon colored. Gradually stir about one-quarter of the hot mixture into the yolks; add this to the remaining hot mixture in the double boiler, stirring constantly until the yolk mixture thickens, about 4 minutes. Remove from the heat and gently stir in the butter, coconut, the 1 teaspoon of coconut extract, and the vanilla extract. Pour into the prebaked pastry shell.

In the work bowl of a stand mixer with the whisk attachment, on high speed, beat the egg whites (at room temperature), add the cream of tartar and beat until foamy. Gradually add the remaining sugar, 1 tablespoon at a time, beating until stiff peaks form. Beat in the remaining coconut extract.

Spread the meringue over the hot filling, sealing to the edges of the pastry. Bake at 350°F for 12 to 15 minutes, until golden brown. Let cool to room temperature, then chill before serving.

COTTAGE CHEESE PIE

SERVES 8 TO 10

1/2 cup plus 1 tablespoon sugar

3 large eggs

1/2 cup half-and-half

2 tablespoons all-purpose flour

2 teaspoons freshly squeezed lemon juice

1/8 teaspoon salt

2 cups cream-style cottage cheese

1 (9-inch) pie shell, unbaked

1/2 teaspoon ground cinnamon

Preheat the oven to 350°F. In a blender, combine the 1/2 cup sugar and the eggs and process for 15 to 20 seconds, until well blended. Add the half-and-half, flour, lemon juice, and salt; process for 15 to 20 seconds, until smooth. Add the cottage cheese; process until smooth. Pour into the pastry shell. Bake for 40 to 45 minutes, until set. Combine the 1 tablespoon sugar and the cinnamon; sprinkle over the pie while warm.

MAMA'S PIE CRUST

MAKES 2 (9-INCH) SINGLE-CRUST PIES

2 3/4 cups all-purpose flour, sifted

1 teaspoon salt

3/4 cup shortening

5 tablespoons cold water

Combine the flour and salt. Cut in the shortening with a pastry blender or 2 forks until the mixture resembles coarse cornmeal. Add the water, 1 tablespoon at a time, until the mixture forms a ball (you may not use it all). Divide the dough in half, cover in plastic wrap and chill for 30 minutes. Roll out on a lightly floured surface and place in 2 (9-inch) pie plates, crimping the edges decoratively.

You may make these up in advance and they can be frozen for up to 3 months.

LEMON MERINGUE PIE

SERVES 8 TO 10

2 cups sugar

1/3 cup cornstarch

1/4 teaspoon salt

1 1/2 cups cold water

1/2 cup freshly squeezed lemon juice

5 large eggs, separated

2 tablespoons salted butter

2 teaspoons grated lemon zest

1 (9-inch) pie shell, prebaked

1/4 teaspoon cream of tartar

1/2 teaspoon pure vanilla extract

Preheat the oven to 350°F. Combine 1 1/2 cups of the sugar, the cornstarch, and salt in a large, heavy saucepan. Gradually add the water and lemon juice, stirring until the mixture is smooth. In a medium bowl, beat the egg yolks until thick and light yellow; gradually stir into the lemon mixture. Add the butter and cook over medium heat, stirring constantly, until the mixture is thickened and bubbly. Cook for 1 minute, stirring constantly. Remove the pan from the heat and stir in the lemon zest. Pour the filling into the pie shell.

In the work bowl of a stand mixer with the whisk attachment, on medium-high speed, beat the egg whites and the cream of tartar until foamy. Gradually add the remaining 1/2 cup sugar, 1 tablespoon at a time, beating until stiff peaks form. Add the vanilla, beating until combined. Spread the meringue over the hot filling, sealing to the edges of the pastry. Bake for 12 to 15 minutes, until the meringue is golden brown. Serve at room temperature.

PUMPKIN CHIFFON PIE

SERVES 16 TO 20 / MAKES 2 PIES

3 1/2 cups cooked or canned pumpkin
    purée
1 cup firmly packed light brown sugar
1 cup plus 2 tablespoons granulated
    sugar
Salt
3 tablespoons light molasses
3 tablespoons bourbon or dark rum
    (optional)
3 teaspoons ground cinnamon

1 teaspoon ground ginger
1/2 teaspoon ground nutmeg
1/4 teaspoon ground cloves
4 egg yolks
1 cup heavy cream
3/4 cup whole milk
5 egg whites, at room temperature
2 (9-inch) deep-dish pie shells,
    prebaked
Whipped cream, for garnish

Preheat the oven to 450°F. In a large bowl, combine the pumpkin purée, brown sugar, the 1 cup granulated sugar, 1 teaspoon salt, the molasses, bourbon, cinnamon, ginger, nutmeg, cloves, the 4 egg yolks, cream, and milk. In the work bowl of a stand mixer with the paddle on medium-high speed, beat the 5 egg whites until foamy; add a pinch of salt and continue beating until soft peaks form. Gradually add the 2 tablespoons sugar, continuing to beat on medium-high speed, until stiff peaks form. Replacing the work bowl with the bowl of the pumpkin mixture, or using a hand mixer on medium-high speed, beat one-quarter of the whites into the pumpkin mixture and fold in the remaining whites. Spoon the mixture into the pie shells, filling only to the rim of the pans.

Bake for 15 minutes. Reduce the heat to 375°F and bake for 15 minutes. Reduce the heat again to 350°F and bake for 15 minutes, or until a tester inserted into the filling 2 inches from the edge of the pie comes out clean. Turn off the oven, leave the door ajar, and let the pie stand for 30 minutes longer. Serve warm or cold. Garnish with whipped cream.

RHUBARB-STRAWBERRY PIE

SERVES 8 TO 10

3 cups rhubarb, peeled and chopped

1 cup sliced strawberries

1 cup sugar

1/2 teaspoon grated orange zest

3 tablespoons all-purpose flour

Pinch of salt

1 (9-inch) pie shell, unbaked

2 tablespoons unsalted butter, cut into
   small pieces

Preheat the oven to 400°F. Combine the rhubarb and strawberries with the sugar, orange zest, flour, and salt. Pour the filling into the pie shell and dot with the butter. Bake for 40 to 50 minutes, until the filling is set.

Favorite Diners

The Dalai Lama at Mary Mac's

September 6, 1995, was a particularly extraordinary day at the restaurant, filled with the topic of Tibet, not to mention a spiritual wonder. The Dalai Lama ate lunch at Mary Mac's during a visit to Atlanta on a twelve-day tour of America. After speaking at Emory University and visiting the tomb of Martin Luther King Jr., he dined with actor Richard Gere at the tea room. The Dalai Lama (who's not a vegetarian) began his meal with "pot likker" and cornbread and went on to sample the fried chicken, while John personally prepared a meal of vegetarian marinara sauce over pasta for Gere. After lunch, as the two special guests led the way to the door with entourage in tow, the customers in the hall fell silent and parted to form a lined exit. Suddenly, the Dalai Lama stopped unexpectedly in front of a stunned server, smiled, and rubbed the server's elbow. No words were spoken, just a quiet occurrence that wasn't scripted or predicted. That very evening, the same server was in a motorcycle accident. As he and his bike fell, his elbow was the center of impact in the accident. He was completely uninjured.

BROWNIES

MAKES 30 BROWNIES

3/4 pound (3 sticks) salted butter, softened

3 cups sugar

6 large eggs, lightly beaten

1 1/2 cups plus 2 tablespoons all-purpose flour

1 cup cocoa powder

Pinch of salt

1 cup chopped pecans

1 1/2 teaspoons pure vanilla extract

Preheat the oven to 350°F. In the work bowl of a stand mixer with the whisk attachment, on medium speed, beat the butter and sugar until light and fluffy. Add the eggs, beating well. Combine the flour, cocoa powder, and salt in a small bowl; add to the butter mixture, mixing well. Stir in the pecans and vanilla. Spread the batter into a greased and floured 18 by 12-inch sheet pan. Bake for 30 minutes. Let cool completely before cutting into 30 squares.

CHOCOLATE FUDGE POUND CAKE

SERVES 12 TO 16

3/4 pound (3 sticks) unsalted butter, softened

5 cups sugar

5 large eggs

3 cups all-purpose flour

1/2 cup cocoa powder

1 teaspoon baking powder

1/4 teaspoon salt

1 1/8 cups milk

1 tablespoon pure vanilla extract

Preheat the oven to 300°F. Butter and flour a 10-inch tube pan. In the work bowl of a stand mixer with the whisk attachment, on medium speed, beat the butter and sugar. Add the eggs, one at a time, beating well after each addition. Sift together the flour, cocoa, baking powder, and salt 3 times. Combine the milk and the vanilla. Add the dry ingredients and milk mixture alternately to the egg mixture, beginning and ending with the flour. Pour the batter into the tube pan. Bake for 1 hour and 20 minutes. (The cake will not be completely set and will wiggle a little when you remove it from the oven.) Let the cake cool completely in the pan.

"Have you tasted one of my desserts yet? Honey, you're really not livin' right if you haven't."

—SHIRLEY MITCHELL, cook

EGG CUSTARD

SERVES 8 TO 10

6 large eggs

1 cup sugar

4 cups whole milk

2 tablespoons unsalted butter

Pinch of salt

2 teaspoons pure vanilla extract

Ground nutmeg

Preheat the oven to 300°F. Butter a 2-quart baking dish. In the work bowl of a stand mixer with the whisk attachment, on medium speed, beat the eggs until foamy; add the sugar and beat well.

In a heavy medium saucepan over medium heat, bring the milk just to a boil (small bubbles will form around the rim; do not boil). Remove the pan from the heat and add the butter, salt, and vanilla, stirring until the butter melts.

Slowly pour the milk mixture into the egg mixture in the mixing bowl. Beat for 2 minutes; pour into the baking dish. Place the baking dish in a larger baking dish and place the pans in the oven. Pour boiling water into the outer dish until it comes about halfway up the sides of the inner dish. Bake for 1 hour and 15 minutes, or until a knife inserted into the center comes out clean. Sprinkle with nutmeg.

CREAM CHEESE POUND CAKE

SERVES 10 TO 12

This is my mother's recipe and is wonderful served with fresh, seasonal fruit and topped with whipped cream. But I prefer it sliced and toasted in the morning for breakfast.

1 (8-ounce) package cream cheese, softened

3/4 pound (3 sticks) salted butter, softened

3 cups plus 3 tablespoons sugar

6 large eggs

3 cups all-purpose flour

1 teaspoon pure vanilla extract

1 teaspoon pure lemon extract or almond extract

2 pints fresh strawberries, hulled and quartered

Whipped cream, for garnish

Preheat the oven to 300°F. Lightly grease a Bundt pan. In the work bowl of a stand mixer with the whisk attachment, on medium speed, beat the cream cheese and butter for 10 minutes, or until creamy. Gradually add the 3 cups sugar and beat for 5 minutes. Add the eggs, one at a time, beating just until the yellow disappears. Gradually add the flour, beating on low speed until blended. Fold in the vanilla and lemon extract. Pour the batter into the pan and bake for 1 1/2 hours. Let the cake cool in the pan; remove from the pan and let cool completely on a rack.

Place the strawberries in a large bowl. Add the 3 tablespoons sugar and toss until the sugar dissolves, about 2 minutes. Cover and chill for at least 1 hour or overnight. Stir occasionally. To serve, spoon the berries over slices of the pound cake and garnish with whipped cream.

PEANUT BUTTER PIE WITH CHOCOLATE CRUST

SERVES 8 TO 10

This is one of our most popular desserts, no doubt because of the chocolate-cookie crust. If you liked Oreos as a kid, you'll love this grown-up pie.

5 cups crushed chocolate crème-filled cookies

3 tablespoons unsalted butter, melted

1 3/4 cups sugar

4 (8-ounce) packages cream cheese, softened

1 cup creamy peanut butter

3/4 teaspoon pure vanilla extract

1 egg yolk

1 1/3 cups heavy cream

Whipped cream, for garnish

Preheat the oven to 300°F. Butter a 9-inch pie plate. Combine the crushed cookies and the melted butter until thoroughly blended; press evenly in the bottom and up the sides of the pie plate.

In the work bowl of a stand mixer, place the sugar and add the cream cheese and peanut butter. With the whisk attachment, on low speed, beat until fluffy and well blended. Add the vanilla and egg yolk and mix well. With the mixer running, slowly add the heavy cream and beat until blended. Pour the batter into the pie shell. Bake for 45 to 60 minutes, until a tester inserted in the center comes out clean. Chill before serving. Garnish with whipped cream.

PECAN PIE

SERVES 8 TO 10

It's not often that something so simple could be so good. Pecan pie is one of those simply delicious Southern addictions.

3 large eggs

1/2 cup sugar

1 cup light corn syrup

4 tablespoons (1/2 stick) unsalted butter, melted

1 teaspoon pure vanilla extract

Pinch of salt

1 cup chopped pecans

1 (9-inch) pie shell, unbaked

Preheat the oven to 350°F. In the work bowl of a stand mixer with the whisk attachment, on medium speed, beat the eggs just until the yellow disappears; add the sugar, syrup, butter, vanilla, salt, and nuts. Pour into the pie shell. Bake for 50 minutes.

Favorite Diners

Richard Gere

When the actor dined with us in 1995, Marion Mims, a "newcomer" at Mary Mac's—she had only been serving customers for ten years—was his server. Never bashful, Marion knew that Gere had just gone through a divorce, so she offered him a marriage proposal. He told her he'd "get back to her." Thank goodness he still hasn't gotten back to her, since Marion's customers would be disappointed if she up and moved to Beverly Hills! Marion has a big heart and warm personality. Gere could have done worse!

"Martha and I went to school together in Crawfordville, Georgia, and when Martha moved to Atlanta and started working here in 1973, she told me how much she liked it. I moved to Atlanta and came to work at Mary Mac's in 1975, and we are both very popular waitresses these last thirty-five years. We like to make our customers feel good!"

—EVELYN STEWART, left, and MARTHA EVANS

SWEET POTATO CAKE

SERVES 10 TO 12

1 1/2 cups canola oil

3 cups sugar

4 large eggs, separated

1/4 cup hot water

2 1/2 cups sifted cake flour

1 tablespoon baking powder

1/4 teaspoon salt

1 1/2 cups raw sweet potatoes, peeled and
   grated

1 cup chopped walnuts or pecans

1 (8-ounce) can crushed pineapple,
   undrained

1 teaspoon vanilla-butternut flavoring

8 tablespoons (1 stick) salted butter

1 (12-ounce) can evaporated milk

3 egg yolks

1 cup sweetened shredded coconut

Preheat the oven to 350°F. Butter and flour the bottom and sides of 3 (8-inch) round cake pans.

In the work bowl of a stand mixer with the whisk attachment, on medium speed, combine the oil and 2 cups of the sugar and beat until smooth. Add the 4 egg yolks, the hot water, cake flour, baking powder, and salt and beat until well combined. Stir in the grated sweet potatoes, nuts, pineapple, and vanilla-butternut flavoring.

In the clean work bowl of a mixer with the whisk attachment, on medium-high speed, beat the 4 egg whites until stiff; gently fold into the batter. Divide the batter among the 3 cake pans and bake for 25 to 30 minutes, until a tester inserted in the center of the cake comes out clean.

To make the frosting: Melt the butter in a small saucepan over low heat. Add the evaporated milk, the remaining 1 cup sugar, and the 3 egg yolks and stir well. Cook for about 12 minutes over medium heat, stirring frequently, until the mixture is thickened. Pour the mixture into the work bowl of the stand mixer, with the whisk attachment, on medium speed, add the coconut. Beat the frosting for 1 to 2 minutes, until cool.

Let the cakes cool in the pans; transfer to racks to cool completely. Spread the frosting in between the layers and on the top of the cake.

I would like to thank the following people who have helped in the creation of this book: Rebecca Lang, Gregg Bauer and Carol Armstrong of MAX20 in Atlanta, photographer Brad Newton, Hank Thompson, Bridget Chandler, Liz Kenemer, Judge Dorothy Beasley, Max Cleland, Steve and Marie Nygren, Marsha Reinle, Celia Keeling, Buena Frisbee, Gweneeth Conklin, Nancy Shaidnagle, Gene Luckey, Lee Fields, Mike Fuhrman, Derek Banks, Martha Wilder, Margaret Wingate, Kelly Stringer, David Stringer, Ronnie and Delores Spears, Billy Sherrill, Joe Patton, the Georgia Tech guys, Tommie Nichols, Tony Totis, and the entire staff of Mary Mac's Tea Room.